"My Dear Child . . ."

Also by Colin Urquhart:

WHEN THE SPIRIT COMES
MY FATHER IS THE GARDENER
ANYTHING YOU ASK
FAITH FOR THE FUTURE
IN CHRIST JESUS
HOLY FIRE
THE POSITIVE KINGDOM
RECEIVE YOUR HEALING
LISTEN AND LIVE
PERSONAL VICTORY

"My Dear Child . . ."

Colin Urquhart

Hodder & Stoughton

LONDON SYDNEY AUCKLAND TORONTO

British Library Cataloguing in Publication Data

Urquhart, Colin
  My dear child.
  1. Christian life – Devotional works
  I. Title
  242

  ISBN 0-340-53642-X

Published by Hodder and Stoughton,
a division of Hodder and Stoughton Ltd,
Mill Road, Dunton Green, Sevenoaks, Kent TN13 2YA
Editorial Office: 47 Bedford Square, London WC1B 3DP

Photoset by Rowland Phototypesetting Ltd
Bury St Edmunds, Suffolk

Printed in Great Britain by Clays Ltd, St Ives plc

To Anthea
and all those who,
through this book,
will hear the Lord say:
'My dear child . . .'

Contents

Acknowledgments

It is no exaggeration to say that the experience of writing this book has changed my life. I have received so much from the Lord and cannot adequately express my thanks to him.

Anthea, my secretary, has done far more to assist than type and retype the text. She has helped considerably with the editing process and I am grateful for her sensitivity to the Lord and her devotion to the task. She has been on the receiving end of the revelation God has given, and her life has been changed as a result.

My thanks also to Laura who has collated the scripture references, and to Katya.

Of course, this book could not have been written without the loving support of my wife Caroline, my family, and all at Kingdom Faith Ministries.

A Word of Explanation

This is a book written from the Heavenly Father's heart to the hearts of his children. Obviously it is not scripture, nor is it in any way intended to stand alongside the Word of God in significance.

Prophecy is one of the gifts of the Holy Spirit: God speaking into the lives of his people. So this book is a form of prophecy, and I believe many will experience God speaking to their hearts concerning issues which are of deep and immediate concern to them.

To write this book the Lord asked me to draw aside for several days to listen to what was in his heart. The experience of doing this has changed me as a person in many respects. I have a clearer understanding of who God is and of the nature of his love for each of his children. This is reflected in the text of this book, and I believe you will receive a greater revelation of God's love for you as you read it.

The Lord wanted to open his heart to me about himself, revealing several aspects of his nature – not only his love, grace and mercy, but also his wrath, justice and judgment.

The Lord asked me to write this book at a time when I had not made provision for writing in my full schedule. But the impact of what he has said has made this task a joy and not a burden. I count it a great privilege to have been called aside by the Lord to spend this time with him and to be his 'mouthpiece' in writing this book. He has greatly encouraged me in faith and love by what he has said.

The form of the book is simple: God is speaking to 'My dear child'. This child is a believer in the Lord Jesus Christ and is in a personal relationship with him, and therefore with the Father. My prayer is that you will hear his voice in these pages and will meet personally with your Heavenly Father as a result.

This book is ideally suited to use during your daily time with the Lord. It could also be used in a prayer group. In either case, you will find it helpful to read the text aloud. The language has deliberately been kept conversational in style.

I have spent time listening to him every day for over twenty-five years. Paul warns us that our prophecy is imperfect, and I have done my best to keep the human element to a minimum. Of course it is impossible to eliminate this completely, because in prophecy God is speaking through an imperfect channel. But nothing would be gained by trying to put my own ideas or opinions into his mouth!

An appendix of scripture references relevant to each section is included for your study. This is only a small selection of the scriptures that could be quoted. I have also made an audio cassette tape of readings from *My Dear Child* . . . and this is available from:

Kingdom Faith Ministries,
Roffey Place,
Crawley Road,
Faygate,
Horsham,
West Sussex RH12 4SA

Please accept this book as a contribution to your spiritual life from a Christian brother who has sought to hear the Father honestly and convey what is on his heart. May you rejoice eternally in his love.

May your roots go down deep into the soil of God's marvellous love; and may you be able to feel and understand, as all God's children should, how long, how wide, how deep and how high his love really is; and to experience this love for yourselves, though it is so great that you will never see the end of it or fully know or understand it. (Eph 3:17–19, Living Bible)

Colin Urquhart

1

I Have Personality

———— o ————

My dear child, I created heaven and earth. Many have wondered how creation came into being. For me it was simple. I spoke. This is all I had to do. Whatever I speak comes into being; it happens. Can you imagine the creative power and energy of my words?

Yet I am not a man; I am Spirit. People think of spiritual forces as powers which have no personality, like the wind. I am an almighty, powerful Spirit who has personality.

My power is only used in relation to my character. I am love and I have the power to create. Put the two together, and you can see that I create in love. You must understand that there are no other creative forces. **I am the only Creator.** This is another way of saying I am the only God. Men have always tried to imagine what I am like and have had all sorts of wrong ideas. They have created gods according to their own understanding. Clearly this is false and shows how important it is to know me, the only true God.

Throughout the centuries I have spoken to men and women to show them what I am really like, and this is why I am speaking to you now.

This earth is but a minute part of what I have made. But I love this planet and all I have made to live on it, including you. At first there was no life on the earth, so I set about bringing form and order. If you look at creation, you will see how orderly it is, how carefully I have planned and made things.

I won't dwell on the details of the plants and animals because I want to concentrate on you. Yes, I made you. You are only one of millions, I know. Yet because I have made everything in love, I have made you in love. You may not understand what this means, but you will.

The word that comes out of my mouth has personality. This word can express everything I am. It expresses my love, my life, my joy, my power, my will – everything about me. There is nothing about me that cannot be expressed through my word.

Why should this be so important for you to understand? Because a day came when the personality of my word took human form. This word, my creative word, became a man and lived among other men.

Do you know what this means? It signifies that, although I created the entire universe, I decided to become a man for a short period of time. I had very good reasons for doing this, as you will see.

During this time, I didn't cease being God. No, there could never be a time when I didn't exist. I continued in the full personality of my spiritual life and power; but the word through which I created became a man so that everyone could hear my voice clearly. Yes, I wanted to speak to everyone, to show men and women what I was really like. I wanted them to understand why I had created them, what in their lives pleased me and what grieved me.

Those who please me are truly happy. But those who disregard me can never experience real fulfilment in their lives. They become frustrated and fearful.

2

In My Image

—— ∘ ——

My dear child, I have made you in my image. This does not mean you are exactly like me, but you are to reflect my character and personality. Whatever I am, I want to see reflected in you. **I see you as the real master-work of my creative ability.**

I have made mountains, rivers, seas and trees, animals, birds and fish. But I have not made anything else like you. You see, all the other aspects of my creation can give me glory by being what they are. However, I can be glorified by you in a very particular way.

Animals can't have a loving, spontaneous, joy-filled relationship with me like you can.

3

No Accident

———— o ————

I created you in love, for love. Isn't that good? My real expectation is that you will know my love, be filled with my love, express my love, return my love, give my love to others and enjoy my love. My whole purpose for you is centred around love. Always remember this.

When I created, there was no order on the earth. I enjoyed bringing order out of chaos and seeing everything come together as I had envisaged in my mind. When you look at the creation around you, you can see how ingenious I have been. I have created order in everything from a snowflake to a leaf, from the limbs of an animal to your brain, heart and every other part of your body. No man could have devised or thought up such a scheme of creation, let alone produce it.

I laugh at those who say it is an accident. Accidents end in chaos, confusion and disaster. No accident ends in such finely planned and thought-out order. Deliberate action on my part was at the inception of everything.

So, my child, you were no accident. **You are part of my overall plan.** Sometimes you think that if it had not been for a man and a woman making love, you would not exist. But who made that man and woman? Who made them able to have a sexual relationship? Who had oversight of your birth?

When you were a young baby you were not able to think, understand and believe as you can now. But I have watched over you and am bringing to fulfilment my plan for your life.

I am a most extraordinary inventor, aren't I? Even when things appear to go wrong, I am able to work in the situation. I can turn everything to good for my purposes.

4

Created In Love

———— o ————

My dear child, I am your Almighty God, and I am your Father. I love you.

I know your understanding of words such as 'Father' and 'love' are coloured by your experience. But my heart is not like that of any human father. My love transcends any other. You can't judge my love by human standards, no matter how good your experience of love.

You see, my child, before the world was created, I knew you. I appreciate this is impossible for you to understand fully. But I don't dwell within the limitations of time; I am eternal. I am able to see the beginning and the ending of all things at any given moment.

So, **even before you were born, I knew you.** From the moment of your conception I have watched over you. I have seen your conflicts, turmoil, trauma even. I know your fears, your sins, inadequacy and insecurity. You have often wondered why I made you in such a way if I truly loved you. But I didn't make you like that. **I made you to be like me.**

I knew I would draw you to this moment when I could speak to you heart to heart. I want to explain my love to you in such a way that you can experience that love and be set free from all the things that have made it difficult, impossible even, to reflect my love in your life.

When you lose sight of my love for you, real problems arise. Sadly, some of my children do lose sight of the centrality of my love, and become hard-hearted. I want you to enjoy your relationship with me, child. Then you will always respect me as your Creator, the Holy One who is Almighty.

Because I created you in love, I had to give you free will. This means you are able to hate as well as love, to be selfish and proud if you wish. Everybody has been created with the ability to choose what to do and how to behave.

You are no exception. Because you have free will, you have the ability to respond to my love. Many choose not to do so, but that doesn't stop me loving them and longing for them to be set free from the things that deny my love. I would like everyone to know and enjoy my love and express this in their relationships.

My child, this is what I want for you.

5

My Plan for You

———— o ————

Before creation began, I decided to have a number of people like you who would be my children, and respond to my love. Out of the chaos and confusion of their lives I decided to bring my divine order to prepare and equip them for heaven.

This is no small task. At first everybody rebels. They sin and are cut off from my love. **I sent my Son to restore them to relationship with me.** As soon as they give their lives to Jesus, my divine order for their lives is established. My Holy Spirit works in each of my children to bring my plan to fulfilment.

So, my dear child, this is what is happening in your life. **You will be transformed into my likeness, changed from one degree of glory to another.** You will one day see me face to face. Then you will be like me, and you will reign eternally with me in glory. I am looking forward to that so much. I want you to look forward to that time, my child. Please co-operate with me in all I need to do in preparing you for this.

You will share my sadness for all those who are unconcerned about my reason for creating them. They want to make their own way through life. Sadly, if they decide to do without me now, they will do without me eternally. If they look to their own works for salvation, their own works will have to save them. This is impossible, isn't it? Nobody can know the glory of my heaven through their own works.

6

My Way of Salvation

—— ∘ ——

I was not taken by surprise when man sinned. I had already planned what I would do when this happened.

Some people talk as if I was taken by surprise and had to alter my strategy to bring men back on course. How mistaken they are. They don't understand that I live in eternity and can see the end from the beginning. I knew very well what would happen.

Like everyone else, you fell short of my glory and what I wanted for you. You were proud and selfish, wanting your own way.

So, my dear child, **I planned for Jesus to take all your sin, failure, fear and inadequacy to the cross. I sent him to take your punishment so that I would have no cause to be angry with you. His blood and your faith have saved you from my wrath. He died for you so that you could have a new life, and become a new creation.** I needed to liberate you from spiritual darkness and make you a child of light. The only way for anyone to know me is through Jesus. This is why you have had to put your faith in him, and all he has done for you.

My dear child, I am so pleased you have done this. Now you and I can have a great life together.

7

I Care for You

———— o ————

I didn't create you to suffer at the hands of others, although I knew this to be inevitable. My Son, Jesus, was subjected to opposition, rejection, abuse and hatred. I allowed this because I love you so much.

You see, my dear child, I wanted to free you from the effects of sin, failure and fear. **I wanted you to be able to receive my life,** a life so real and full that you could allow yourself to love and be loved without fear of hurt or rejection.

Jesus had to be vulnerable in the same way as you to make this possible. As I have watched over you and seen the hurts that have accumulated, I have longed to bring you close to Jesus. For if you are close to him, you are close to me.

So don't think I have been unconcerned about your needs. I have been waiting for you to give me the time and opportunity to set you free from the things that have caused the shame and hurt you have experienced.

I have spoken to you in love many times. Often you've pushed away what I have said. I've spoken to you through others, but you've refused to listen. So I rejoice that now you will sit at my feet and allow me to give you understanding of my love. **I want to speak from my heart to your heart.**

8

You Are Saved

——— o ———

My dear child, I have saved murderers, prostitutes, drug addicts, alcoholics and criminals. Don't you think I am able to save you? I have saved people from communism, hinduism, buddhism and many other 'isms'. Don't you think I can save you?

Why do you always think you are the difficult one? Why do you think it should be more difficult for you to receive from me than anybody else? Why do you give the impression that Christ died for everybody else except you? This doesn't seem to make any sense. You suggest I have one law for everybody else, and a different one for you. I am allowed to bless, heal and save others, but not you.

You keep saying to yourself that there is nothing special about you. Yet you treat yourself as a special case, as if you are the only one I cannot forgive, heal, save or liberate.

I think it's time for you to repent of your pride, don't you? You think such attitudes are the fruit of being humble; but they are not. You are saying you know better than I do! I know more about this salvation business than you!

If you confess your sins, I am faithful and just to forgive you and cleanse you from all unrighteousness.

Believe what I say. I am faithful and just. I have forgiven you and cleansed you from all unrighteousness.

Accept that you are saved because you have asked me to forgive you and you have put your faith in Jesus. You are accepted by me.

Begin to look at yourself as I see you, instead of telling me you are not what you are. You even suggest I couldn't do for you what I have already done. It's very frustrating being your Father if you don't believe my love, and question my goodness and generosity to you!

9

Let Me Love You

———— o ————

I will always speak to you in human terms you can understand. I want to draw you close to me, child. As your Father, I want to hold you in my arms. I won't force myself on you. There have been times when I wanted to enfold you in my love, but you pushed me away. So I've had to be patient, waiting for the time when you would be prepared to open yourself to me, when you would dare to trust me enough to let me love you.

When you receive my love, you know my peace. Then you begin to experience the joy of being loved by me. Instead of feeling vulnerable, you have a new security.

You have feared what people would think if they knew you loved me. Such concerns don't matter. Your need of my love is much more important than other people's reactions, wouldn't you agree?

You have also been slow to believe the reality of my love for you. Many of your fears have been the result of your doubts.

Trust me. I want to teach you how to rest in my love without thinking you have to do something to deserve it. This doesn't seem right to you, does it? But you cannot earn my love, and you don't have to; I already love you.

So enjoy my love. Because I love you, I enjoy you. Why do you find this difficult to believe? **I want you to enjoy me.** I want you to know times when you can rest in my love and enjoy me.

To you this seems like selfish indulgence; yet this is the greatest need in your life. Don't you see that the more you allow yourself to rest in my love, the more able you are to take my love to others? Often the love you have given others has been frantic, not a resting, trusting love.

You don't need to justify my love for you; and you don't have to be afraid to entrust yourself to me. You've really longed to know my love for you, haven't you? My child, as you learn to find time to rest in my love, so you will be able to take that rest into every other area of your life. In the midst of all your difficulties, you will be able to trust in me and know the love I have for you.

10

The Lost Child

———— o ————

A child sat in tears in the middle of the crowd. She was lost, separated from her parents. Some walked past unconcerned. The child didn't belong to them so they ignored the problem.

Then someone went up to the child, took her by the hand and tried to console her. At first the child wouldn't respond because this was not her mother or father. She gave no answer to the questions but continued to sob uncontrollably.

Then from the crowd appeared a distraught mother who enfolded the child in her arms. The sobbing gave way to cries of relief from both mother and child. She lifted her up, hugging her closely, assuring, soothing.

My dear child, do you ever feel lost in the crowd? Others may try to soothe you, but I am the only one who can lift you up and meet your need.

11

I Love You Because I Love You

———— o ————

My love for you does not depend on your performance or achievements. **I love you because I love you.** I have called and chosen you. You have been afraid to come closer to me because of your sense of inadequacy; but **I want you close to me**. I like you.

You have often thought it's my divine job to love you because I am God. But you have doubted that I really like you. You see so many things about yourself you don't like, things you know are not my will for you. If you don't like yourself because of these things, you have concluded that I don't like you either! I haven't liked your sin, which is why you have felt uncomfortable when you grieved me. But I don't love you only when you are good. I don't love you only on your obedient days. I love you because I love you; and I like what I am doing in your life.

I like to bring about changes which free you from the things you don't like about yourself. I like to see repentance which leads to forgiveness and a release from your guilt. I like it when you become less religious and more loving! I like you, my child. I really like you.

12

I Love You More Than You Love Yourself

———— o ————

Don't you realise, child, **I love you more than you love yourself**? I like you more than you like yourself. I am more patient with you than you are with yourself.

What do you think I should do with you when you step out of line and disappoint me? What should I do when you deliberately avoid what I am saying, and blind yourself to the truth? Should I punish you? Should I push you away from me because you no longer deserve my love? Do you think my love is only for good, perfect people who always obey me? If this was the case, I wouldn't have anyone left to love!

Imagine a mother holding a young baby in her arms. Does she ask for her child to be perfect, mature and obedient immediately? She knows the child will need training, teaching and discipline. When he learns to walk, he will touch what he shouldn't touch and do what he shouldn't do. He will show little discernment as to what is right or wrong.

But the mother doesn't reject her child, saying she cannot love such a disobedient failure. No, she draws the child closer, saying to herself, 'I will train him and love him and discipline him when necessary. He will grow up to be a fine boy.' And she will defend him against any who criticise him. He is so precious to her.

Hear my father's heart beating as I tell you these things. Don't you see that this is how I regard you? I know you haven't reached perfection and maturity; you are still learning to walk in my ways and do what pleases me.

You are like that small child. You are hurt by doing things you shouldn't, aren't you? This is the way you learn. **It is in your own best interests to do what I say.**

My child, my love for you is not a passing or fleeting infatuation. I have committed myself to you, to love you, to be faithful and true to you through all phases of your growth and training. I have promised to bring you to maturity and to the fulfilment of my purposes. I will bring you to perfection, but I don't treat you as if you are already perfect!

13

Don't Be Afraid of Love

—— ° ——

I don't like all I see in you now, because I am righteous; but I have you in hand.

Sometimes I touch vulnerable areas of your life and you want to wriggle free from my grasp, at least for a while; you feel the pressure is too great. No sooner have you shaken me off, than you long to be in my arms again! You miss the comfort, strength and peace of knowing my presence with you. Slowly you learn to submit to me and my ways. At first you obey me begrudgingly, but later you rejoice in doing what I ask of you.

There are still areas of your life that you consider to be your own. Either you've not submitted these to me, or you've felt that I am not interested in your weakness and need.

I haven't touched those parts you've not wanted me to touch. I have respected your free will and waited for your invitation.

I am able to heal the delicate wounds inflicted by others in the past. My touch is not like their touch. Their touch has hurt you; **my touch will heal you.** Trust me.

Every way in which I touch your life will be for your good. Even when I discipline you, it is always in love. You don't have to shield yourself from me. I don't withdraw from you, but continue to hold you until you relax and are ready to receive from me.

Why be so tense, my child? Why keep from me what is mine? I love you, every part of you. **I don't love an image of what you ought to be, but you; the person you really are, with all your faults and failings.**

I assure you of my love. Nothing is hidden from my sight. I wait until you allow me to touch those vulnerable areas of yourself from which you have excluded me.

14

I Am Gentle With You

———— o ————

Why do you imagine that my touch will hurt and wound you? I am gentle. I want to touch you with my tenderness. I care about you and deal lovingly with you. I don't work in your life by wounding you, making further healing necessary. **I want to heal you through the revelation of my love.**

I enjoy tender moments with you. I want you to give yourself time to enjoy me. Please don't come rushing in and out of my presence in prayer, without letting me speak lovingly to your heart. I encourage those I love. It's not my purpose to destroy you, but to build you up in faith.

I came as one who served. I came to wash the feet of my disciples. Many of my children find it difficult to let me serve them by washing their feet. They must always serve me rather than me serve them! They fail to realise that unless they receive from me, they cannot give to others. Living in fellowship with me doesn't mean you have to strive to accomplish things all the time.

My dear child, learn to be still and know that I am God.

People imagine I break hard hearts through violent action, judgment and punishment. No, I break hard hearts by melting them with my love. So I keep loving and loving and loving, no matter what response is given me.

Understand then, my child, there is never a moment in time when I don't love you. You are the apple of my eye. **You are one in whom I delight.** I can never love any of my children with anything less than a perfect, unchanging love. I embrace you in love, in whatever way is right for you at that time. **You are never out of my thoughts.**

15

I Am Your Father

———— o ————

My child, don't judge me by your human experience of a father. Your natural father was a man and failed in many ways. You were aware of his weaknesses as well as his strengths.

Some people have suffered rejection at the hands of their human fathers because they were men who could not be trusted. They were unjust or unconcerned about their children. I never abuse my children. **I am near to all who call on me.** I am never distant. I comfort, strengthen and heal them. So I am not to be compared with any other father.

I am not a man. There are no weak, vulnerable areas in my life. There is never inadequacy in me, or inability to meet a need. I love you with my everlasting love that will never fade; it will never be withdrawn from you. As your Father, I watch over your development and I am concerned to protect you from things that are dangerous and harmful to you.

You haven't always heeded my warnings; so at times you've been hurt. But I have always been on hand to heal you and meet your need. Sometimes you've allowed me to do this; at other times you haven't.

I never deal with you as you deserve, but only with compassion and grace. This is difficult for you to understand. I give and give and go on giving to you. I never come to the end of my giving.

You often think to yourself, 'Who am I that I should receive such love, that I should know the personal affection of my God?' You are fearful that my love might suddenly be withdrawn and then you would feel rejected. If you were to open yourself fully to me and then I turned away, you would be devastated. But I would never treat you like that.

I don't withdraw my love. I don't commit myself to you only for a set period of time. My commitment to you is unending, as a commitment of love must always be. Love cannot be real if it is suddenly withdrawn.

I already know you, every part of you – and yet I love you. I see what you try to hide from me. So, hiding is futile. I will not stop loving you because I uncover some unsavoury part of your character. My love for you is real. It doesn't depend on who you are but who I am!

16

You Make It Difficult for Yourself to Receive Love

———— o ————

My dear child, when you accuse, judge and condemn yourself, instead of believing what I say, you find it difficult to receive my love, don't you? You concentrate on your inadequacy and problems, wondering if it could be true that I love you.

You've listened to the enemy sometimes, haven't you? He tries to sow seeds of accusation in your mind and encourages your sense of inadequacy, making you feel unworthy of my love. Don't be deceived by any of his tactics. He is a liar. He has no right to accuse you.

I don't regard your inadequacy and failure as the truth about you. The truth is that I love you. You are precious in my sight and I honour you. I see you as one who is slowly but surely responding to me, whose heart is being melted by my love. I see you as my child belonging to my family, made acceptable to me through the blood of Jesus.

You could do nothing to deserve my love; I am so much higher and greater than you. So why not accept the fact that **you can never earn my love, only gratefully receive it?** My dear child, I don't disapprove of those who approve of me! If I did so, who would be left for me to approve? Don't think I regard you in the same way as I regard those who still belong to the kingdom of darkness. The enemy shall not have you. The destroyer shall not touch you, for you are mine.

Sometimes you are concerned because I give you so much, and you give me so little in return. This is *false* guilt. One of the most loving things you can do for me is to allow me to give to you in the way I choose. Then many others will receive my love through you, if you are to love them as I love you.

As a channel of my love you will radiate my love in your character and actions.

17

I Love the Person You Really Are

———— o ————

My child, I am never deceived by appearances. You find that disconcerting. There have been many times when you have put on an appearance for my benefit or for others. You have tried to be what you know you ought to be. But it has never worked, has it? **I see through the barriers and behind the masks you wear.** So why imagine they make you more acceptable to me? I don't accept you because of any of that. None of those masks encourage me to love you any more than I do already. They only make it more difficult for you to receive my love.

I love the person you really are. I sent my Son to die for the real you – not some superficial, false expression of who you are. I don't like masks and barriers. I love people. I don't love what they ought to be; I love them as they are. You have vainly imagined that the masks would be more acceptable to me than the reality of what goes on inside you. I look at the heart. I know the longings of your heart and the conflicts also. You give people the impression you don't need to be loved; but I know differently. You try to persuade others that you are fine as you are. You are able to cope, even though often you feel so lonely within yourself.

I love to come behind the masks and barriers to touch the lonely with my presence, to touch the fearful and inadequate ones with the assurance of my love. You have always feared, my child, that I would reject what lay behind the mask; but this is not true.

I come where nobody else can come. I am Spirit, and I come into your spirit and fill you with my love and say to you, 'Don't be afraid. There is nothing to fear from me.'

18

You Don't Need to Pretend

—— o ——

My dear child, why are you so concerned about what others think of you? This occupies so much of your time and gets you into pitiful muddles, doesn't it? Others have the same problem about you. They wonder how you regard them. And I watch all this going on.

Everybody wonders what others think of them. I see them fencing and sparring with one another and they become defensive and fearful. If only they would be open and honest, they would be so much happier. They would discover that they don't have to put on a performance for one another.

Are you listening to me, child? This is very relevant for you, isn't it? **Be yourself and stop trying to be someone else.** Then life will be so much easier for you. You imagine that if anybody knew you for who you are, they would reject you. So the somebody else you try to be is rejected, because everyone knows this is not the real you!

I know who you really are, and I accept you.

19

Your Appearance

———— o ————

My dear child, you spend a lot of time being concerned about your appearance. I like you to look clean and presentable. When Jesus walked about on earth he didn't go around dirty and scruffy. Neither did he wear his best suit all the time.

But, my child, you spend so much time preening the outside, while I am concerned with what is on the inside. It doesn't matter how smart or expensive your appearance, if your heart is poverty stricken! When my love shines through your life, it doesn't matter whether you are wearing your pyjamas, jeans or your best clothes.

Sometimes I look at congregations of smartly dressed people in church and I think to myself, 'Who are they trying to fool?' They say they put on their best clothes for me. The best clothes they could wear for me are a pure heart and a good conscience. These delight me.

Those with pure hearts and clean hands ascend the hill of praise, holiness and true worship. So, present your body as a living sacrifice, holy and acceptable to me. Even your best clothes wear out, but a pure heart doesn't; it is eternal.

My dear child, I wish you would spend as much time being concerned about your heart as your appearance. I

say this gently to you, but it is something you need to hear.

You are often complaining you are the wrong shape. This makes me smile. I see people doing all kinds of things to change their shape. Sometimes it is important that they do, especially if they are guilty of gluttony and are overweight in a way that affects their health. But they would be much healthier if they were more concerned about their spiritual weight and shape!

My Spirit lives within you to encourage the right priorities in your life. So let's work on these things together, shall we? We'll get things in right order. You can look forward to the day when people will be glad to see you because I shine out of your life. Then they won't even notice what you wear, or your shape. What a day that will be, my child!

20

The Real You

———— o ————

My dear child, I think you are beautiful. I really mean that. You are beautiful because you are made in my image, to reflect my glory. I can see my life in you, emerging like a butterfly from a chrysalis. Soon you will be able to spread your wings and fly freely.

Many of the ways in which I touch your life are apparent to others. But nobody else can see those deeply personal times we have together when you shut yourself away in your room to be alone with me.

Do you remember what I promise? I will reward you openly for what I see in secret. At such times you can bare your most intimate thoughts. You can tell me how you really feel. **I never mind, child, what you share with me.** The more open you are, the better I like it. The more real you are, the more I can respond.

This is much more meaningful than formal times of prayer, when you say things you think I want to hear which don't come from your heart. **I want to relate to the real you.**

21

Our Prayer Meetings

—— o ——

Often you need assurance that I am pleased with you. But I am not only pleased with you when you feel the closeness of my presence. Have you ever been in a room with someone you love and yet it is not the appropriate time to hug or kiss them? You can communicate your love in other ways, can't you? It's the same when we are close. Sometimes it is right to enfold you in my love but at other times I want to communicate with you in other ways. I may need to reveal my thoughts to you and give you wisdom.

It would be very boring if every time you drew aside with me the experience was the same. Have you noticed in your relationship with other people, you cannot always predict what they are going to say or do? It is the same with me. I'm not predictable, am I? I don't dance to the tune of any of my children. **There is glorious variety in the ways I meet with you.**

When you don't feel I am close to you, I haven't deserted you, nor have I failed to turn up for the prayer meeting. I certainly haven't taken you off my popularity list. You can always rejoice, whether you feel my presence or not.

Listen child, I am never late for a prayer meeting with you. I am always there before you are, waiting for you to come. You know, sometimes I've been disappointed because you haven't shown up. Does that surprise you?

22

Be Open

—— ○ ——

My dear child, it is good to talk things through with me, isn't it? Then you let me into the secret places of your heart. You have the spiritual need to open these areas to the influence of my Spirit. When you are open about these hidden things, I can deal with them. Don't say, 'Oh, you know all these things, Lord.' **Take the trouble to tell me about them, and you will experience great release.** Then the enemy cannot take advantage of you in these areas.

While you try to work out things for yourself, he tries to take advantage, doesn't he? I watch what goes on in your mind. You go round and round in circles. The enemy goes round in those circles with you. He tries to increase the confusion.

I never go round in circles. I always come straight to the point and lead you to the answer, child. So when you share your inner turmoil with me, that is the beginning of the end of it; even though it takes time to unravel because you have been in a spiral of confusion.

23

Give and You Will Receive

―――― o ――――

We are going to have some good times together in the future, aren't we, child? You have been longing to know what is on my heart. Well, you see, **when you share with me what is on your heart, I share with you what is on mine.** You have to share with me first.

The measure you give is the measure you get back. This is a principle of my Kingdom. I am not going to change my principles for you, or for any of my children. Share your heart with me and I will share my heart with you.

24

No Fear in Love

—— o ——

My dear child, there is no fear in my love. My love casts out all fear. You have prayed about your fears and have asked to be set free from them, haven't you? The only way for this to happen is for you to receive my love. Then the fears flee away. In receiving my love, your healing is accomplished, and you are set free from the things that have caused the hurt.

The way you find it most difficult to receive my love is through others. Because my love is born of the Spirit, you want to receive it directly from me as a spiritual experience. This is good; but it's not the only way in which I communicate my love to you.

My Spirit of love lives in others. Just as I want to express this love through you to them, so I express this same love through others to you. But you find it hard to receive in this way because you fear you will be in debt to the one from whom you have received.

What you fail to understand is that **you are also reluctant to receive love from me, because this places you in debt to me.** Better to be independent and self-contained, for then you will not need to be in debt to anyone, even me! But I don't love you to place you in debt or bondage. I love you because I love you. I don't express my love to you through others to place you in debt to them, but because I want to break down your stubborn self-will and independence.

It is humbling, isn't it, to discover your need not only of me but of others also? It is humbling to realise that you cannot fulfil my purposes by being independent and self-contained.

Sometimes you have argued that to receive love from others makes you vulnerable to them and open to hurt. So you have said, 'Better only to receive love from God directly.' Then what will you do with all the love I put within you? Are you going to refuse to give it to others in case they are threatened by your love?

When you experience my love, you want to communicate it and give it to others, don't you, my child? If everyone was like you, afraid to do so, who would receive my love?

There is always a vulnerability in love and the possibility of being rejected or hurt. But because my love is born of the Spirit, that love brings healing. If someone who has communicated my love then hurts you, I will always send someone else to love you and be my instrument of healing to you.

25

You Are Accepted

—— o ——

Sometimes the enemy attempts to make you feel guilty at having received so much from me. He suggests that it is not your place to receive, only to give. So he encourages you to chase around in a frenzy of constant activity, lest you be rejected by me for doing too little. Even when I encourage you to be still, to receive and rest in me, he suggests that unless you are constantly active you cannot be in my will. Don't listen to such lies.

My child, as you learn to rest in me, your tensions and anxieties ease. You cease to strive. When you believe that I accept you, it becomes evident that you don't have to try and earn my favour. I want you to work because you know you are already in my favour.

You don't have to try to make yourself acceptable to me. You are already accepted because you have put your faith in what Jesus has done for you on the cross. There he dealt with all the unloving things about you – every sin and failure. **Every fear and every need was met.** It is pointless to try to make yourself acceptable when you already are! Believe what I have done for you and live in the good of it.

There is no point in my giving you tender assurance of my love if you don't believe what I say. I have demonstrated my love, not simply by words, but in action. In giving my Son's life on the cross, I showed the full extent of my commitment to you. I was prepared to love you even to the point of death.

26

I Watch Over You

—— o ——

My dear child, I knew you before you were born. You were an object of my desire and my love, even when I planned your life. You wonder how this could be true as you are only one of a multitude of people.

I see the deliberate disobedience of many. **But in every generation I have planned that there will be those who are my own special possession.** They fulfil my heart's desire and radiate my glory in their lives.

You are such a one, child. I watched over the circumstances of your birth, your parents and your family. You wonder at that because things have been far from perfect in your childhood and adolescence. There have been many difficulties and traumas. Did I plan these?

Well, my child, I saw you through them all, didn't I? Those difficulties were important in building your character and in teaching you to look to me and depend on my love. It is quite painful growing up, isn't it? All those tensions you had to go through, and the questions. This is an inevitable process. You had to go through it; but look at you now! You have a heart full of love for me and the rest of your life stretches before you. You can love and serve me for the rest of your life, and you will be with me in glory for evermore. This is comforting to know, isn't it?

Don't fear what is ahead of you. **If I could see you through past problems, I can certainly see you through future experiences.** I have seen new life emerging in you through all these developing processes. Since you put your faith in Jesus, my Spirit has been producing fruit in more and more areas of your life.

I watch this process and it really delights me. You have no idea how it thrills my heart. I love to see myself reflected in my children. This causes them to be really happy and fulfilled.

I love to see my joy breaking through in you. You are learning to rejoice in me, even when things seem really tough. I have been good to you, haven't I?

27

People

——— ० ———

Do you know what I like to give you? What you have been most afraid of – people. You see, I love people. I draw my children together in genuine unity. You can be thankful for the friends I have given you. **I want to give you relationships in which you can know my love and unity.** I am present in a very special way among those who love me. I have many more people to give you in the coming years. You can show how much I care for those I bring across your path. You can speak my word into their lives. Others I will bring into your experience as ambassadors of my love to you.

Sometimes others attack and hurt you. I don't want this. But I forgive you when you hurt others, don't I? And I forgive them when they hurt you. I want *you* to forgive them. I won't forgive you if you refuse to forgive others. When you forgive, **I am present to heal the hurts inflicted on you by others.**

Do you remember when it seemed everybody turned against you? You thought the enemy was working through everyone. You hardly knew which way to turn, did you? So you turned to me and I saw you through. I provided for you, precious child. Those past hurts do not seem nearly as significant now, do they? I am still undoing their effects so you can walk in greater liberty.

I like the way you are learning to have real faith about the future, to expect good things. You are not so afraid of the people you meet and the way in which you have to relate to them. This is good, real evidence of my work. You have been able to trust me this far; so trust me for the future.

28

Every Detail

———— o ————

My dear child, I know how many hairs you have on your head. If such a minor detail is known to me, don't you think that more important things about you interest me? You have often thought that I am not concerned about small details because I'm so busy looking after everybody else.

When my Spirit comes to dwell in one of my children, every thought, problem or need is of personal concern to me. This is why you can ask me for anything in the name of Jesus and I will give it to you. It doesn't have to be a big need, but any little thing that worries you.

Some people ridicule those who learn to trust me for little things. They suggest I couldn't be concerned with petty matters. But they are wrong. My love for you is such that I don't regard anything as petty. **If you regard something as important enough to pray about, I regard it as important enough to answer!** Some don't receive because they don't ask. They could receive so much more from me if they only trusted me for small matters.

Don't listen to those who laugh at you because of the way you depend on me. I love you, child. I love to do things for you. I won't allow you to be idle. I won't do for you what you are supposed to do yourself. I am teaching you to be a responsible disciple.

You and I have a love relationship. **Just as you love doing things for me, so I love doing things for you.** It has taken ages for you to appreciate this. You used to be surprised when I did anything for you! Now you are beginning to see the point. You and I can live together in love every day.

29

I Lead You Step by Step

——— o ———

My dear child, sometimes I have asked you to do difficult things. At least, they seemed difficult at first and so you were reluctant to respond. Trust me, do what I say and later you will understand my wisdom.

If I had shown you the whole picture at the beginning, you would have tried to produce the end result in your own way, instead of letting me lead you step by step. On other occasions, if I had shown you where I was leading you, you would have refused through fear. **I work in your heart to prepare you for what lies ahead, changing your mind and desires.** As my will unfolds, you are prepared to accept the next step. Then, when you come to the end of the process, you have a great sense of fulfilment because you know you have done what I asked.

When you look back over this whole process, you marvel at how much I have actually done within you. This sense of fulfilment in knowing you have obeyed me and completed my purpose is my precious gift to you, my child. Sometimes you wonder whether you got everything right. Time and time again I assure you, 'That is good, my child. You have done what I asked.' Even before I send you, I know what you will say and do. I take all that into account.

You get all hot and bothered about things when you listen to the enemy who tries to give you a false sense of failure. Don't allow him to do this. I enjoy what I am doing in you now, despite the fact that sometimes you flounder. **I will enjoy leading you to a further stage of maturity, growth, development, fruitfulness and glory!**

I will enjoy each stage along the path. As far as I am concerned, the whole process is to be an enjoyable one. I don't place false expectations on you. I know what I can expect of you at every stage along the way. What I ask of you now, you are able to fulfil now. A little while ago that would not have been possible, but I have prepared you. My timing is always perfect.

30

Don't Worry About the Future

——— o ———

The future is going to be exciting, child. You don't have to know the details. Many of my children want to know everything that is going to happen to them. I can understand their concern, but I want them to trust me and be content that my word is a lamp for their feet. I will take care of their tomorrows. If they obey me step by step, I will look after them.

Take no thought for tomorrow. Each day has enough cares of its own. The way I programme your life means that each day will have enough for you to contend with; but if you take other burdens about the future on yourself, you will carry a load too heavy for you. Then you will begin to feel unable to cope.

If you can't deal with what is happening now, you won't have much motivation to allow me to lead you on. So it is very important for you to obey me by not worrying about the future.

When I speak to my children to give them direction, I do so in a variety of ways, once even through a donkey! I always ensure they hear me.

I know how to speak to every one of my children. Why should I speak in ways you can't hear?

Sometimes I have to listen to the frustration of those who think I have forgotten them. They have heard nothing more from me because they need to obey what I have already said. When people don't like what I say, they wait for me to say something else. No wonder they get stuck!

But you are not like that, child. **You hear my voice.** You are learning to discern the difference between my will and the spoiling tactics of the enemy. That's good, because I don't want him to distract you.

My sheep know my voice and follow me. You are one of my sheep, child. You know my voice and I rejoice that your heart is mine and that you want to follow me.

31

All of Me

—— ○ ——

My dear child, how much of me do you possess? **All of me.** You wonder how you could possess all the love of your God, for I have so many others to love as well. But I don't love anybody the way I love you. My love for you is utterly unique.

A human mother and father may have several children, yet love each one with all their hearts. They won't divide their love into portions, giving one part to each child.

I don't divide my love into millions of segments and say to you, 'Here, my child, have one small portion of my love.' No, I give you all of my love. I give you all of myself; I love to live in you by the power of my Spirit. Isn't this wonderful?

I speak many truths into your heart to show you how precious you are to me. Live in the fullness of the glorious inheritance you have through Jesus.

32

All of You

—— o ——

I have another question to ask you. How much of you belongs to me? Everything. **All of you.** You are mine for ever.

I have paid the price for you, haven't I? I didn't purchase part of you with my Son's blood. I purchased the whole of you because I wanted every part of you. So you really are my property, child.

How much of you do I possess in practice? I know every part of you belongs to me, but do you really surrender every part of yourself? Do you still want your own plans and purposes, instead of mine? You know the answers, child. **But just as I am encouraging you to take possession of every part of me, so I am taking possession of every part of you.**

With the blood of my Son I purchased the freehold of your life and I have entered in to take possession of every part of my property. Yes, my child, every part.

I want all of you, not part of you, in heaven. So I am taking possession of what is rightfully mine. Most of the time you enjoy this and co-operate with me, but sometimes, child, you hesitate, don't you? You like the idea of belonging to me completely, but you don't always want to face the practical implications of this, especially when I ask you to do something you don't want to do. I am patient with you at such times. **When you acknowledge that what is mine is mine, then all conflict raging within you will cease!** You will be at peace again. Have you noticed that the more I have possession of you in practice, the happier you are? Do you know why? Every part of you that I take possession of becomes filled with my life, love, joy, peace and power. Why withhold anything from me then, child?

Some try to hold on to their money. They are afraid to let me use it because they think I will take it all from them. They don't believe that whatever is given to me, I measure back abundantly. So if they don't let me have their money, they miss an area of my abundance. Sad, isn't it?

Are you glad I have been patient with you, child? Have you noticed, beloved one, that **the more you let me possess you, the more of me you possess**?

33

I Am Merciful

———— o ————

My dear child, I am merciful: slow to anger and quick to love. You are a branch of the true Vine, Jesus. In my love I prune *every* branch to make each one more fruitful. When I apply my pruning knife to your life, I cut away the superficial.

I have not allowed unrefined parts of your life to interfere with our relationship, or with what you have been able to receive from me. This is an aspect of my mercy for which you need to be thankful.

You wonder how I could have blessed you so much when you have doubted me, questioned my love, disbelieved my word and promises. In my mercy I deal with these things so that the quality of our relationship will be enhanced. **I don't try to deal with everything that needs to be corrected all at once.** I maintain my steadfast love to you despite all these things.

34

True Liberty

———— o ————

Sometimes you experience liberty when you focus on me with praise, only to return to your struggles afterwards. I want you to know liberation which lasts. You are still unaware of many of the things I need to deal with. My mercy will remain new to you every day so that your fellowship with me will not be hindered while I am dealing with you.

Some people give an impression that everything is fine and such a process is not needed in their lives! How foolish and deceived they are.

Most of the pain and fear of the refining process is only in your attitude. When I do the work, it is gentle, isn't it? It is loving, tender and gracious. This is the nature of my heart.

So don't hide your need in praise. Don't pretend everything is fine when it isn't. Trust in my mercy to deal lovingly with you, and encourage others by assuring them I am merciful.

Be very thankful when others express my tenderness and loving forgiveness, when they are compassionate and show the understanding that comes from my heart. You need to pray, my child, that more people will reveal the true nature of my heart, not in harsh judgment, but in tender care.

I am always merciful to those who fear me and to those who are concerned to walk in my ways. Because I am rich in mercy, I have made you alive with Christ. I want you to be rich in mercy, too. **You are merciful by nature, child, because Jesus lives in you.**

35

When I Forgive, I Forget

———— o ————

My dear child, *everybody* needs to be loved. They need to know that I accept and approve of them. You can be an ambassador of this truth to many other people when you believe that I have forgiven and accepted you.

When I forgive, I forget. **Through Jesus' sacrifice your sin is put away from you, and from me, for ever.** So when I look at you today, I don't see you in the light of your past sins and failures. As far as I am concerned, those things no longer exist. It is as if they never were.

Still, you sometimes feel condemned by your past. On one level you accept that I have forgiven you, but on another you don't believe that my forgiveness could be so thorough and so easily obtained. You find it hard to see that I will never hold these things against you. I want to assure you now of the real nature of my forgiveness.

I honour the sacrifice of my Son. **So I forgive you completely.** He suffered the punishment you deserve. You are free from guilt, child, because I have forgiven you. You are free from condemnation because you belong to me.

36

Forgive

——— o ———

As I have forgiven you, so I want you to forgive others. Forgive those who have wronged you. Forgive those who have denied you love, or have suffocated you with it. Forgive those who have brought condemnation upon you. Forgive as I have forgiven you.

Every time you forgive, fresh resources of my love will be released in you. **Your heart will be kept tender with my love.**

The more you understand my heart, the more you will appreciate how much it grieves me when you don't forgive. I have shown you such mercy that it offends me if you are ever unmerciful. But it causes me joy when you forgive. I love to see myself expressed in you.

37

The Fight

——— o ———

A group of children were playing together. Their game became more and more boisterous. Before long, tempers became frayed and an argument started. Each thought he was right and refused to yield ground to the others. When they returned home, each child looked battered and bruised.

'Just like children – always arguing!' said one mother.

'You wretched child, look at the state of you,' said another.

'I hope you gave as good as you got,' said one father.

'Don't let anyone get the better of you,' said another.

Then one wise father said, 'Child, forgive.'

38

Love is Patient

———— o ————

My dear child, I have had to be patient with you and **I want you to be patient with others**. You're not always, are you?

Just as I have to make room for your mistakes, so you have to be tolerant towards others without judging or condemning them. I have to be patient with you while you learn; so you have to be patient with them while they learn. You are more patient than you used to be, aren't you? But I think you notice some room for improvement!

You know, **love is not proud.** Pride is often the cause of your impatience. You think others ought to do things as you do them, and see things as you see them.

I give you revelation, child. You must be patient with those who have not received the same revelation. Sometimes they judge you, don't they? But don't judge them in return. Be patient with them.

39

Love Does Not Boast

———— o ————

You can boast about me, child, but not about yourself. **Love does not boast.** Everything I give you is a gift of grace. Everything I do through you is the fruit of my Spirit. All these things are done for my glory and not for your self-esteem.

Never envy what I do in others. I do quite enough in you to keep you well occupied! So don't be jealous of the way I use others, my call on their lives or the gifts they have received.

40

Love is Kind

———— o ————

S hall I tell you something that really distresses me? I
have a number of children who talk about my love,
but they are very rude to others. They take them for
granted, make them feel small or even ridicule them.
Love is not rude.

Don't be rude, child. You know, one small piece of
rudeness can ruin your witness in somebody's eyes.

It is better to be kind because **love is kind.** I have never
been rude to you, have I? If I had wanted to, I could
certainly have said some rude things about you; but it's
not my nature. I could have scorned, mocked and criticised you if I had been like some people; but I am not. I
am like myself.

Instead of being easily roused to anger, I am merciful,
patient, loving and kind. Because my love lives in you,
don't be easily angered either, even when people do
foolish things.

41

Love Covers Sins Instead of Exposing Them

—— o ——

My love keeps no record of wrongs. I don't keep a record of what I have forgiven. I am not going to produce a catalogue of sins and hold it in front of you, even on the day of judgment. I don't want to remember them. I am only thankful that they are covered by the blood of my Son and no longer exist in my sight. I like to look on righteousness, not sin. On the day Jesus returns, you will stand guiltless before me with others who belong to me.

Another thing that distresses me, child, is seeing people delighting in evil. Some want to join others in their sin. Others delight in uncovering evil. When they do, they make a meal of it. They want to expose their brothers and tell others of their sins. They even claim that they are doing something godly to purify the Body of Christ. I think their actions are despicable. They would not want me to uncover all their sins and parade them in public.

The measure anyone gives is the measure they get back. When people gossip and expose the sins of others, it is only a question of time before their own sins are exposed, unless of course they repent. I hate such actions because really those children of mine are rejoicing in what is evil. They are taking every advantage of it. True love is saddened and grieved at discovering evil.

Love covers a multitude of sins. It does not expose them. I want you and all my children to rejoice in the truth, not in what is evil. I want you to delight in those who do my will and be thankful for every expression of my life you see in others.

Love always protects. So if you love your brother, you will always protect him. You will never expose and criticise him before others, or listen to criticism of him from others. Your love of others will always protect them. My father-love for you always protects you.

I planted my love in you so that you can always protect those whom you love. My love does wrong to no one. Others will value my love in you when they see that protective quality being expressed.

42

My Sin Record

———— ◦ ————

43

Your Sin Record

———— o ————

(Once you have been forgiven)

44

Love Never Fails

———— o ————

Love always trusts. Yes, always. If you love me you will always trust me. I want you to prove trustworthy to others.

My love always hopes. This means you can look to the future with positive attitudes, knowing that my promises will be fulfilled. I speak of future events with as much certainty as if they had already taken place.

Don't give up. Persevere, holding on to my word with an honest and good heart. Believe the promises I give you and continue in the glorious hope to which you are called.

You are going to see me face to face, child. You are going to have a new resurrection body. You will live in glory with me. This is your hope.

Love never fails. I will bring you to the fulfilment of all these aspects of your hope. I will not fail you, and I don't want you to fail others. Honour your word to them, just as I honour my word to you.

My love will never pass away. Do you realise, my child, my love for you will never end? And neither will your love for me!

45

Trusting Others

—— o ——

My dear child, I know you find the whole business of trusting people confusing. Others are only trustworthy when they abide in my love. **I can trust you when you abide in my love.** I know then that you will fulfil my purpose and do what I say.

I am not asking you to be foolish. Be wise as a serpent and innocent as a dove.

You know by the witness of my Spirit within you when people are not trustworthy, just as Jesus did. He didn't put his confidence in man. So my Spirit will give you the witness, child, of when it is safe to trust people and when you need to be wary of them.

Jesus didn't entrust himself to any man. You must love those you doubt are trustworthy, like he did. But don't make yourself vulnerable to them. It is dangerous to be vulnerable to critical, strong-willed, independent people. They are not to be trusted. They will hurt you and cause unnecessary damage in your life.

Put your confidence in me, my child. I will always give you the relationships you need where you can share your heart with others and it will be safe. Those with whom it is safe are those who abide in my love. Trust me. **I will show you how to love each person I put before you.**

46

I Have Chosen You

———— o ————

I call you 'child' because this is what you are: my child. I have called you by name and made you mine by my decision and choice. You have responded to my love, but I took the initiative.

This is still a wonder to you, isn't it? **My love for you is not sentiment. It produces positive results in your life.** You are no longer the person you were. You are a new creation, a child of my grace. I give to you because I have chosen to do so.

Sometimes, my dear child, you feel ashamed because you know you do not measure up to what I want. So you are reluctant to draw near to me in case I reprimand you. And yet **when you do turn to me, you are always met with love, never with harshness.** Have I ever given up on you? Have I ever rejected you, or turned away because you were in disfavour with me? No, my child. I maintain my love to you. It is a steadfast, sure and certain love that will never fail.

Yes, there are times when I have needed to discipline you. There are times when you have not known the closeness of my presence because you have chosen to walk in your ways, and not mine. But I have never withdrawn myself from you. I am with you always, as I promised.

47

I Discipline in Love

———— o ————

My dear child, I discipline in love. But you must understand that my purpose is not always to discipline you. I only do this when necessary. I much prefer to encourage rather than discipline.

I discipline you only when you have been really sinful and rebellious, doing deliberately what I told you not to do. You have stubbornly refused to repent. Then I have had to make you aware that I am the holy God; I am your Lord and you must not treat me or my word lightly.

But when you think back through your life since I became your Lord, there have been very few occasions like that. I very seldom need to punish you and, even when I do, I only take measures that are absolutely necessary to break you of your stubborn self-will and bring you back to obedience to me. **Any loving father punishes his child when necessary.**

Do you realise, my child, that if you are seeking first my Kingdom and righteousness, I certainly will not have any cause to punish you? Instead, my promise is that everything will be added to you, which is totally the opposite. You usually realise when you are at fault and I can easily correct you. When things are not right between us, my Holy Spirit makes you feel uncomfortable. Usually you take notice of what I say, even though it may take a little time. Sometimes the flow of blessing in your life dries up for a while. This is not punishment, but discipline to bring you back to the place where I want you to be.

I only exert pressure on your life when it is for your own good. In all things I am working for your good. **I redeem the testing times and turn them to my advantage and yours.** You don't always appreciate that at the time, do you?

48

I Encourage Your Faith

———— o ————

My dear child, the trying times build and encourage your faith for they teach you how to rely on me. I prove that I will never fail you or leave you, no matter what the situation.

Sometimes there are stubborn problems in your life; it seems that no matter how much you pray about them, they persist. But I am the God of perfect timing. I know precisely when and how to meet with you. Have you noticed how many times you have been in the right place at the right time to hear a particular message, and my Spirit has moved in a way especially relevant for you? These things are not coincidental. They are not accidents. They are evidence of the way in which I plan the details of your life.

I want to lead you and provide for you, but you don't always listen to what I say. I give you a simple command and you question whether you are able to hear my voice so distinctly. Do you think I want to make it hard for you to hear me? Why should I do that? I know how to speak to you, and I am teaching you to recognise my voice.

Faith comes from hearing me. But how many times have I spoken to you and you have not heeded what I said? Later you have thought, 'That must have been the Holy Spirit!' I want you to realise, my child, that **you do hear my voice.**

I don't nag at you like the enemy does. That persistent nagging never comes from me. I gently speak my word to your heart. The enemy shouts at you and tries to drown out my voice. You don't have to listen to his shouts; listen to my still, small voice.

49

You Can Do What I Ask

———— ○ ————

It is easier for me to hear you than for you to hear me. So why think I don't listen to your prayers? Do you think I am too busy? Or do you imagine you are not sufficiently important for me to take notice of you? Could anyone be more important to me than one of my children, whom I have adopted for myself?

I don't know of anyone more important than you! Does that surprise you? Well, it shouldn't, my child.

You see, I consider each of my children important. One is not more important than another to me, because I love each one equally. So stop thinking you are unimportant. I don't like it when you think you are of little significance.

I want to do big things *in* you. I want to do big things *with* you. You find that hard to believe, don't you? You know why? You are afraid of failing me. You fear that you will not hear me correctly, or if you do, you will get it wrong.

Don't you think I know my business, child? If I am the Lord Almighty, would I ask you to do something that would cause you to fail? I am not like that. **I want to see my children succeed.** I wouldn't ask you to do anything too hard for you; I would choose someone else instead.

You see, I am the finest personnel officer; I always appoint the right person for the right job.

Often your first reaction is to think that what I ask of you is impossible, because you know these things could not be accomplished with your natural resources. But whatever I ask of you is possible because I have given you my Spirit. **Everything is possible if you believe.** You believe me, don't you, child?

I know your capabilities. Don't think I only look at you as having potential. The thing I like about you is that you are realised potential. I can see the fruit I have produced in your life. This gives me glory! Yes, child, you give me glory!

50

I Never Despair of You

———— o ————

My dear child, have you noticed how tender my love is for you? So why fear punishment from me? Why fear you will meet with my disapproval if you fail? At times you are disappointed with yourself, child. But I have never despaired of you. I know when you are going to fail.

It is true that I have disapproved of some of the things you have done and said, but **I don't disapprove of you.** You are too precious to me. Sometimes you feel out of sorts spiritually, emotionally or even physically. Almost your first thought is to ask yourself what you have done to cause my disapproval. Oh, my child, this is no way to live.

You can be out of sorts with yourself, but this doesn't mean you are out of sorts with me. In fact, usually when you are like that, I am there with you, waiting for you to turn to me and receive my tender love. When you do, you realise you have been worrying about nothing.

51

My Love Makes You Clean

———— o ————

My dear child, I want to enfold you in my arms of love. I draw you close to me. It is my pleasure. Would I have called and chosen you unless I wanted you? When you held back in fear, I gently persisted. If I hadn't, you would have missed great blessing, wouldn't you? There is no part of your life, my child, that is not a concern to me. I have promised to sanctify you through and through; spirit, soul and body. I will fulfil that purpose.

My love makes you feel clean. I speak my word of forgiveness to you and you feel clean. I touch your life with my Spirit and you feel clean. I heal you and you feel clean. **Whenever you receive from me it has this cleansing effect on you.**

When you fear, you feel unclean. You cower away, fearing that the problem is in you. You think you are so unclean that you cannot receive my love, blessing and healing.

I want you to *be* clean, *feel* clean and *appear* clean because you radiate my holy life. I can't give you anything unclean. The fruit produced in your life by my Spirit is good, pure and wholesome.

52

I Enjoy You

——— ○ ———

I enjoy you, child. I enjoy knowing you. I enjoy loving you. I enjoy being with you. I enjoy giving to you. I enjoy hearing from you. I enjoy your praises. I am in love with you, child.

53

Enjoy Being You

—— o ——

There are many ways in which I have needed to come deep into your life to liberate you from fear of displeasing me. This is fear of yourself, really. You have been very afraid of yourself, haven't you, child? Can you see the work I am doing in you now, to liberate you from that fear? How can you enjoy being you if you are afraid of yourself?

Precious child, thank you for letting me love you. Thank you for letting me come deep into those secret places. You don't understand all that I am doing in you. That doesn't matter. It's enough to know I understand you, that I heal you and make you whole.

Your days of hiding from me are over, aren't they? You don't need to do that any more, do you? Oh, my dear, dear child. There have been many times when I have longed to give to you, but you have kept yourself out of my reach. How it pleases me that you no longer do that. Not only do you allow me to touch your life with my love but you really want me to. This is a sign of great change in you.

You are beginning to trust my love, aren't you, child? You are beginning to see that there is no need to fear. I always have your best interests at heart, and every touch of my Spirit of love is making you more holy.

I love you, child. There is a sweetness about my peace, isn't there? Have you noticed that you are now able to cope with situations which previously would have caused turmoil within you? This is because you are beginning to see things my way. You have begun to listen to my voice rather than the enemy. In a very gentle way I have moved in your heart so that you yield more fully to me than before. That's good. You can encourage others to open themselves to me, to come deeply into the arms of my love, to receive from me.

54

Receive and Give

—— o ——

My dear child, do you remember when you felt you had to be continually active for me? It made you satisfied that you were doing something for me; but what was the fruit of it all? You will be more fruitful if you abide in me and I in you.

Don't try to impress me or others with your activity or godliness. You are learning the lesson slowly that **when you receive from me, you become more like me.** It has taken you a long time to appreciate that, but I am glad you know it now.

Would you like to be really useful for me? Would you like to know what would really please me, and how you could glorify me? Let me love you, and then love will pour out of you. Let me give to you, and my gifts will pour through you. It is very simple really, isn't it, my child?

Have you noticed that water keeps falling over a waterfall? It never goes upwards. My love keeps falling on you. It is just like that waterfall. I cannot stop it falling on you. It cannot go upwards and leave you. It can only descend on you. Stand under the waterfall of my love, and receive!

55

I Am Gracious

—— o ——

My dear child, I am the Lord who gives and gives and gives. So you are the child who has to receive and receive and receive. I never come to the end of my giving. Even when you think I could give you no more, I shower further blessings on you.

You judge yourself more harshly than I judge you. According to your assessment, you deserve nothing. This would be true except for my grace.

You know, there are few who really understand my grace. Many preach and talk about it. They concentrate on the fact that people are not worthy to receive from me. But I concentrate on the fact that I am always willing to give. That seems much more helpful!

I know my favour is unmerited, but the emphasis needs to be on my favour. I love to give, child. I am never slow to give when the circumstances are right. Isn't that what I promised through Jesus? He says, **'Everyone who asks receives.'** This is true. Have you noticed that often you have not received because you have been reluctant to ask? When you ask and receive, you wish you had asked for much more and received much earlier. Sweet child, you are learning. That is the important thing.

56

Child of My Grace

———— o ————

You are still surprised when I give to you, my child. You consider that I am bound to give you certain things because I am committed to you. But you only expect the minimum to enable you to do my will.

You don't understand that I want to do beautiful things for you because I love you. You don't think you are very beautiful, do you? I am not talking about physical attraction, but about the person you believe yourself to be. You often wonder why I want to satisfy the desires of your heart.

You are a child of my grace. I fulfil the desire of my heart when I lavish my gifts freely on you. I love it when you pray to me with faith and expect me to answer. I love it when you are not overcome by the need but look to me, knowing I will supply because of my grace. I love that, child.

You wonder whether the desires of your heart are the same as mine. Well, consider this. Where did those desires come from? Selfish desires clearly come from you. But where do those other desires come from? Am I not able to form desires in your heart? Doesn't my Spirit create new desires in you?

57

I Am Generous

————— ○ —————

I want you to understand my grace more fully, so you can be gracious to others. **I am generous, the God of abundance.** I give far more than the minimum.

I don't want you to give me the minimum, but the maximum. Don't clock in or out for prayer or loving others. You are my child all the time. Those who are generous are always willing to give, no matter the cost, even if nothing can be obtained in return.

My child, sometimes you hold back from giving because you are afraid, thinking others would not want to receive from you. Sometimes you imagine you would spoil what I want to do. You are mistaken. I am able to work through you, expressing my generosity and love.

Your selfishness has annoyed you, hasn't it? My child, it is a matter of the heart, isn't it? **I am ready to make you generous if this is what you want.** I will keep giving to you, as long as you keep giving to others. The measure you give will be the measure you receive: good measure, pressed down, shaken together, running over.

I am the God of grace and I will give and give and give and give and give, even to you!

58

The Old Car

———— o ————

The young man had lost count of the number of times he had had to fix his old car. One thing after another went wrong and needed attention. Yet what was the alternative? A new car was beyond his means. He could see no way in which to buy one. So he would have to make do with the old, patching it up as best he could–unless someone gave him what he could never afford himself!

59

The Way of Love

—— o ——

When you face difficult decisions and are not sure which way to turn, you can always ask yourself what Jesus would do. **He would always choose the way of love.** You will find that when you face such dilemmas, it will be obvious to you which of the alternatives before you is the way of love.

It is tempting to avoid this way because of the cost. Sometimes, people don't want to get involved or take on responsibility. But no one who lets himself be distracted from the work I planned for him is fit for my Kingdom. Whoever loves me will obey my commands. This means they will choose to love others as I have loved them. You have found the cost of that, haven't you, child?

Sometimes I've been disappointed in you because you have chosen the selfish way and then tried to convince yourself that this really was the right decision. You have never been very peaceful about it, have you? And peace is not restored until you admit to me, and to yourself, that really you made the wrong decision. But I don't punish you for such mistakes; you punish yourself by losing that beautiful sense of peace. I don't have to take any further measure against you. I wait until you return to the path of love.

60

Love in My Name

———— o ————

When you read about the life of Jesus, you are impressed by the way he loved people, aren't you? Have you noticed that he didn't talk much about love; he did it. He got on with the business of loving. To love with my love is not sentiment, is it?

When I call you to love in my name, telling people that you love them is not enough. You need to listen, serve and give to them; you have to care and pray for them. The way you care for others is a measure of your greatness.

They may simply need you to be with them to give them assurance. At other times you will need to reach into their lives with my power, bringing them healing.

You need love mingled with faith, don't you? Love without faith is insufficient. **You need love expressed in faith, and faith that works through love.**

When you reach out to others in my name, take my compassion and the faith that believes I will change their circumstances and meet their needs. This is what Jesus did, isn't it, child? **He was not content to love people in their need; he met their need.**

61

A Heart of Love

———— o ————

It took some time for you to appreciate that you were really involved with Jesus on the cross. I know you understood quite readily that Jesus died for you. But Jesus took you to the cross with him. You have been crucified with him. It is no longer you that live but he who lives in you. The old selfish life is dead and buried. Now you have a new life. Don't look back on the past; it's gone.

Look forward to the future. **You are a new creation, created in Christ Jesus to do good works.** These do not produce salvation; they are the fruit of your salvation.

Many people do things for me, believing this pleases me. But unless my love is the motivating force behind their actions, they are futile. Apart from me you can do nothing. You believe that, don't you, child?

I have given you a heart of love. Isn't that good? I don't have to keep persuading you to love. It is becoming your nature. You can see why I am pleased with you. In more and more situations you instinctively love, expressing the life of my Kingdom on earth. You are part of the answer to the prayer, aren't you? In *you* my Kingdom is coming and my will is being done on earth, as in heaven.

62

Go in Love

———— o ————

L ove has many healing properties. So I want my love to reach where there is fear, hurt and shame.

I see the poor living in hovels, the starving with swollen bellies. My heart reaches out to them and I commission my children to take my love to them. At the same time I see the greed and selfishness in others; my heart is saddened. I see the corruption of those who take for themselves what is intended for the poor, and I am angry.

You live in a world of need, my child. But this does not mean you should be afraid to know my generosity and abundance yourself. I have impressed on you that **the more you receive from me, the more you can give to others.** I have been working in your heart, filling you with my love so that you have the motivation to pour out your life for others. You are to love them as I have loved you.

You are discovering that I give and give and give yet again. This is how you are to love others.

Give in the way I ask. Some I send to the poor and the destitute; some to the rich, to break through their apathy and indolence. I love to go where there is misery. I go in the hearts of those who love me. I go with the hands of those who reach out in my name. I go in the prayers of those who are deeply concerned.

63

I Go in Love

——— o ———

Miracles happen wherever my children go in my name. I love to go among the addicts where there is misery, violence and abuse. **I go in those who pour out their lives for them without holding back because of the cost of such ministry.**

How I desire that more of my children would make themselves available to reach those who are in the depths of misery and futility.

I love to go among the social outcasts, the unwanted and unloved. I love to show them that someone genuinely cares. But I need bodies through whom to work, serve and show the affection that is so needed. I go in the gifts of those who give freely of their substance because they cannot go in person.

I love to go in my children who will show them the way of salvation. I love to go to all these places with my gospel, not just with natural physical help. What has been accomplished if the body is fed but the spirit is left naked; if physical needs are satisfied but sins remain unforgiven?

So I go in those who show my love and concern for spirit, soul and body. When I go in them, all my resources are available to them through the power of my Holy Spirit.

64

I Go in You

———— o ————

I love to work miracles of healing amongst the destitute who look to me as their only doctor or dentist, those for whom I am the only surgeon available. I love to send people of faith who will look to me for their provision in every situation.

I send a people of love who will not mind the cost of declaring my truth, those who will proclaim my word in the face of abuse. They offer my love although they know it may be rejected. Great will be their reward in heaven.

I love to go in those who risk danger to take my gospel to others. I love to go among the oppressed. I love to go into prisons. Wherever there are captives, I want to set them free by the power of my Spirit. I love to go where people recognise their need of me. They want my love, acceptance and forgiveness. Such hearts are fertile soil to receive the seed of my word.

I love to go in you, my child. Oh, you cannot meet *all* this need. Your heart goes out to such people because you share something of my heart. I have seen the desires within you to reach the poor, the lost, the naked and the blind. I rejoice in your genuine compassion.

I delight when I hear you say, 'Oh Lord, I am ready to go if you will send me.' I love to see my children available to me like that. But I can't send you everywhere, child. I have chosen a particular ministry for you. I direct the footsteps of all who yield their lives to me. **I use you in the most effective way I can** so that many will be touched by my love. My wisdom exceeds yours in this.

65

The Right Time

———— o ————

The boy looked up at the mountain. It seemed to tower above him so high, grand and immovable.

'Can I climb this mountain?' he asked his father.

'Why should you want to do that?' came the reply. 'You are too young. You don't understand how dangerous it is.'

The boy was disappointed.

As the years passed, he looked often at this mountain, longing for the time when he would be old enough to make the climb alone. It was a challenge which had to be faced.

One day he set out and began to walk on the lower slopes. It wasn't long before he found the going too hard and had to return home, feeling defeated. His dream was still unfulfilled.

'Why are you looking so discouraged?' asked his father.

'I tried to climb the mountain,' the boy answered. 'But I didn't get very far.'

The father put his arm around his son. 'Didn't I tell you, boy, such high mountains are dangerous and difficult to climb? The task is far too great for someone your age.'

'But I want to climb the mountain,' the boy persisted.

'Then you shall,' said the father, 'but not yet. When the time is right I will guide you, and you will climb the mountain with me. Wait until the time is right, son.'

66

Spread My Love

———— o ————

What matters to me, my child, is that you **spread my love everywhere I lead you.** Give time to those who need time, love to those who need love, money to those who need money, help to those who need help. In all these ways, my child, you will be able to spread my love around you. There is so much need and so few who are willing to face the cost of meeting it.

Do men blame me for the sinfulness of men's hearts, I, who am holy and righteous? Do they blame me for the corruption and abuse of freedom? Do they blame me that men choose to hate instead of love, to be corrupt instead of generous?

I am working in the lives of millions all over the world to right the wrongs that have been brought about by men's selfishness. So my child, I am thankful that your heart is mine and that you are willing to go for me wherever I send you, and do for me whatever I ask of you. Don't be surprised, therefore, if I lavish my love upon you. **For as you give me all you have to give, so I give you all I have to give.**

67

My Kingdom of Love

—— o ——

My dear child, it has been my good pleasure to give you my Kingdom. This is not a place. It is my sovereign reign as King in your life. My Kingdom is within you: I have planted it like a seed in your heart. Contained within that seed is the total life of my Kingdom, all the riches and resources that can develop within you. My Kingdom reflects the nature of the King who rules over it.

My Kingdom is not a matter of talk but of power. This power is not merely a spiritual dynamic that produces miracles; it is revealed in love. Even though you can manifest spiritual gifts, have great faith and demonstrate my power, all these things are worth nothing without love.

My Kingdom is righteousness, peace and joy in the Holy Spirit. When you follow the leading of my Spirit you walk in righteousness, peace and joy. I never lead you to love in wrong ways, by indulging yourself in lust or greed. When people walk in unrighteousness, they lose their peace and joy. **You are an ambassador of my Kingdom of love and power.** I want to express my sovereign reign more fully in your life.

68

You Are Filled With My Power

———— o ————

My dear child, because I am almighty, my Kingdom is a reign of power. Some people wrongly try to separate my love and power; but they belong together.

When Jesus loved people, he reached out with my power. He healed the sick, cleansed the lepers and cast out demons. He even raised the dead on occasions. He performed miracles, turning water into wine, feeding multitudes with a boy's picnic, stilling the raging storm. He even obtained money from a fish.

All these things demonstrate that my love is supernatural. And I express this love through people like you!

My Holy Spirit is supernatural and brings both love and power into your life; he enables you to live the life of my Kingdom. Jesus said, 'You will receive power when the Holy Spirit comes on you.'

So, my child, I want you to realise that you are filled with power. Yes, you really are. You rarely feel full of power, do you? Nevertheless, all the resources of my supernatural power are available to you, and are at work within you.

I have given you power to use in your own life. How can you really move in faith and love unless you learn to use those supernatural resources for yourself? You need to know that I will answer your prayer, that I will heal you when you are sick and provide for you when you are in need.

Those who try to love and serve me without making use of the power I put within them are wasting my resources. They don't listen to my Spirit telling them to use the power and authority I have already given them.

I also give you my supernatural power to enable you to minister to others. Show them how to reach out to me to see their needs met. This is what I want.

I send you into the world in Jesus' name to be like him, and to take his power, love, joy, peace and forgiveness into every situation.

I am glad you see this, child. If you take my love without the power, you can only do half the job.

69

My Power in Love

———— o ————

To take my power without love is no use, either. You may see mighty things happening, but those you help are left with no revelation in their hearts of my love and acceptance.

I have been doing a thorough work in you, my child, teaching you more of who I am and how I work in the lives of my children. I want you to have a balanced ministry. That is a popular saying. Many who talk in this way have unbalanced ministries themselves. They demonstrate little of my power and are weak in supernatural gifts. The only person with a really balanced ministry is Jesus. So I want you to be like him and minister in his love *and* power.

My child, every dimension of my Spirit can flow out of your ministry. **Please don't limit me, but remember to minister my power in love.**

I've taught you much about my gentleness and tenderness. I never want you to lose sight of these qualities. Jesus was gentle and humble in heart, but he still ministered with great power. Some think they will only demonstrate power if they do so loudly and aggressively. But there is great strength in gentleness. Reach out with my supernatural power, knowing my tender touch upon your heart as you do so. You need compassion as well as authority.

70

Not by Might or Power

—— o ——

You know, my child, many of my children say they need more power. But really they need love to release the power I have already given them. The only thing that counts is faith working through love.

Those who want more power to perform spectacular signs and wonders often want to do something really impressive. They think this will give me glory and will be a great example to other people. Of course, it will also enable them to be held in high esteem!

There are times when I do choose to work like that, but often my powerful works are done quietly and unobtrusively. Very few of them are public spectacles. **I will be glorified in every act I perform, and others will not steal the glory from me.**

When people testify to what I've done in their lives, this encourages some to respond to the gospel of my Kingdom. Others don't want to believe, despite the great and powerful signs of which they hear. Many refused to believe Jesus despite the great miracles he performed. The world will not be won by extraordinary signs. In the wilderness, the devil wanted Jesus to do something spectacular to grip people's attention. Jesus refused to be seduced by such an idea.

Don't seek glory for yourself, for I cannot entrust demonstrations of my power to those who will become self-centred and conceited. Their pride gives the impression they are the ones responsible for such miracles. My child, walk in love, faith and power, with the humility and gentleness of Jesus.

71

I Love Working Miracles

———— o ————

Every day I am a miracle-working God. Miracles are not occasional events. I do them daily all over the world.

I like working miracles in you. Ask me for one whenever you have need. If you don't have faith for a miracle, ask me to inspire such faith within you. I am *your* miracle-working God.

72

Let Me Carry the Burden

———— o ————

You have felt defeated when you have tried to take my power to people in great need, those who are crippled and deformed, the blind and those in the depths of depression. You haven't been able to meet their need, have you? You have felt a failure because you know I am almighty and can heal such people. You thought that if you were a better Christian, you would be able to do such things in my name; for if Jesus came into those situations in person, the people would be instantly healed.

But remember this, my child; Jesus didn't heal every sick person when he was on earth. He healed all who *came to him in faith*. This is still the principle by which I work.

Don't take the burden upon yourself. I want to increase your faith and your willingness to see how I can use you. I want you to take my love and power to those desperately needy people. But I don't ask you to take their burdens upon yourself. **I am the one who carries their burdens.** If you go to them in my name, child, then I will always give you the right words to say, the right prayer to pray, and you will see change in their lives. You will not always see dramatic results, however.

It may be that the total need is not met instantly; I don't promise that all the answers to your prayers will be in the form of instantaneous miracles. No, my child, I want to take this false burden of guilt from you.

Go into every situation knowing that you are an instrument of my love and power. You will be fruitful on every occasion if you remember this. Don't set false expectations as your standard. In every situation, **listen to the voice of my Spirit** so that I can make clear to you what I intend to do. You only have to be faithful in doing what I ask you.

Sometimes I use a number of people to minister to one of my children. Each person I send has a distinctive part to play. So take heed to what I say, my child. Then you will not leave with a false sense of condemnation that you are powerless to help. You are not powerless. You can take the resources of my love and power in the way that I teach you.

Of course, my beloved, sometimes you will see mighty things. Give me all the glory for these. But consider this. When you go into a situation and obey the voice of my Spirit, bringing about a small but necessary change in a person, that obedience is as important to me as the times when you stepped out in dynamic faith to see a mighty miracle.

You see, my child, I love obedience. It is the expression of your love for me.

73

Loving Difficult People

———— o ————

My dear child, some people are very difficult to love, aren't they? Especially the demanding ones. They are very insecure, with little assurance of my love and acceptance. Their insecurity produces a pattern of manipulation which usually begins in childhood. They don't expect love from people so they have to manipulate. It's very difficult for them to believe anybody loves them for themselves, even me.

I will send you people to love, but they will never be demanding. In fact, that is how you will distinguish those I send from those the enemy puts in your way to sap your resources of love. Those I send come humbly, sensitive to your needs and aware of the nuisance they might be to you.

Demanding people don't mind how much they drain you or how much time they take. No matter what you give them, they always want more. You give them time and they want more time. You give them love and they want more love. You give them money and they want more money.

Such people will waste much of your time if you let them. They will appear to be better when you have spent time and prayed with them; only to be back on your doorstep a few days later, asking you to go through the whole performance again. Instead of teaching these people to depend on me, you will find that they become dependent on you. They will drain you of all your energy and abuse your willingness to love them.

The way to love manipulative people is by not yielding to their demands. Don't ignore them but love them with my love, not in the way they demand to be loved. This means you must learn to be strong.

You see, manipulative people are very good at accusing Christians, making them feel condemned. They suggest you don't love them enough: 'You don't really care, you don't really want to love me, do you?' Such accusation makes you feel guilty, as if you have failed the test of love completely. You feel you have to go out of your way to show you genuinely love them.

This is yielding to their demands. Manipulation works by creating a sense of false guilt in others. Manipulative people always seem to get their own way, while everybody else adjusts to them.

Love these people, my child, by being strong. Make it very clear that you will not be manipulated by listening to their accusations. I warn you, my child. Such people will not always take kindly to this; they will get angry. They will say that if you don't love them in the way they demand, they will want nothing more to do with you. You will be accused of rejecting them. Remember, I don't accuse my children.

The enemy accuses through other people and even uses scripture to do so. In relationships such as these, there is a spiritual battle. You are not waging war against flesh and blood but against the spiritual principalities and powers. These people are bound. They have no liberty in the Spirit. I love them and want to use you to help them by refusing to yield to their tactics. Manipulative people resent it when others stand up to them, but find a security in those who are prepared to be strong. In their hearts they know this is what they need.

They must repent of their manipulation and accusations. They need to be brought to a true revelation of my love, acceptance and forgiveness, which cannot be earned or manipulated. I *already* love them with a perfect love.

74

Be Really Fruitful

———— o ————

Insecure people don't enjoy a close relationship with me because I won't yield to their demands. They say they love me but you can see the unreality of this by the way they continue to manipulate.

They don't feel my love because they don't believe my love. Do they want to? I mean, really want to. Will they be prepared to submit themselves to me instead of wanting to run their own lives?

Now listen, my child. **I love these people. I want to see my Kingdom firmly established in their lives.** My Kingdom does not work through manipulation. It is expressed through genuine love, righteousness and power. It is planted in them like a seed but is choked by their own selfish desires and the way in which they allow problems to become more important than my Kingdom.

Some people will not let go of their burdens, even though Jesus carried them to the cross. They hold on to their problems as if they are essential to maintain their identity. They talk about surrendering their lives to me while holding back areas for themselves. They say they give their problems to me, but within hours they take them back again. They even suggest that nobody could really meet their need – not even me! They see themselves as unlovable with impossible problems, even for the Creator of the universe. They will tell you that famous men of God have ministered to them and still they are left in their need.

Have you noticed that one manipulative person like this can cause a lot of distress to many of my children? I regard this as a serious problem within my body. Yielding to these manipulative tactics leaves an area of bondage within my body, exhausting and draining my people and deflecting them from my purposes.

Will you heed what I say to you? Will you be strong and stand up to those people in love? When they accuse you, come back to me and let me reassure you so that you don't feel crushed and bruised by what they say. Don't say to yourself, 'I am too weak to stand up to these people.'

My Kingdom is within you, child. My strong love is in your heart and you are able to do what I tell you. So rejoice, because you are not going to be kicked around any more. Your love is not going to be abused or wasted. I am going to put it to the best possible use. I want you to bear *much* fruit.

I am sending you to those who need love and really want to be helped. I need harvesters in my Kingdom, not gleaners! You have made mistakes in the past, haven't you? I don't condemn you for this. The way you acted was full of good intentions; but you can learn from past mistakes, can't you? In future you can be far more fruitful in your loving of people. My love in you is not to be soft-hearted; it is tender, but strong!

75

Give Yourself Time to Receive

———— o ————

It is good that you have these times to hear me speak to you and receive my love. You become so drained and tired, don't you? So many seem to be taking from you. They look to you for wisdom, prayer, ministry, care, service and love. You seem to be giving and giving, just like I do.

I know you receive as you give, but you also need times like this, my child, when you can draw aside with me and do not have to give; you only have to be still and receive. It is good to receive.

You used to feel very guilty about that. Every time you drew apart with me in prayer, you thought you should be giving to me. So prayer became very tiresome for you. After giving to so many others, you then had to pray and give to me. At times your mind was so preoccupied with other people's problems that you wondered where to start.

My child, you need time to receive from me so that then you can give more effectively, even in prayer.

Sometimes you felt so exhausted that you fell asleep while praying, simply because you were relaxing from all your activity. Then you felt guilty and a failure in prayer, didn't you?

Your times of quiet with me are times when I can speak my word into your heart to encourage, refresh and revive you. Then your heart begins to overflow with worship, thanksgiving and praise. Have you noticed that the flow of praise dries up when you are exhausted?

When you have received from me, you can go back into the world ready to give, not resenting the demands made upon you. I am glad, my child, that you are losing that sense of guilt about receiving. Do you remember when you thought you should only receive a little? So many people had given you completely the wrong idea about prayer.

But I have been re-informing you. Let me put it this way, child. What can you give to me that I don't already have? What can I give to you that you need? Well, it is obvious who should be doing the receiving and who should be doing the giving, isn't it?

Your greatest need is to be loved. I am the only one who can meet that need. So relax, my child. Know my love for you. Receive from me and then go out into the world, sharing that love with others who need to receive it.

76

I Heal

——— ० ———

My dear child, I am the Lord who heals. You would think everyone would be happy about this, but they're not; far from it! There are those who claim I don't want to heal, others that I have lost the habit! They believe that although I once healed, now I do so no longer. There are even those who become very angry when I do heal, because this offends their theology!

There are those who say I want to heal some, but not others – as if I view the subject with an arbitrary attitude. Others believe I always want to heal.

Some look for reasons why healing doesn't take place; others speak of my sovereign will, which seems an excuse to believe anything!

It's a very confusing situation, isn't it? Yet to me the matter is simple. So, my dear child, I want you to understand what is in my heart concerning healing. **I heal because I love.** I don't want any of my children to be sick and I certainly don't enjoy seeing them suffer.

Have you noticed, child, that when you are in pain you automatically cry out to me? This is instinctive because you know I love you. When anyone is sick they look to those who love them for support and encouragement.

Of course, it is one thing to cry out to me for help; quite another to believe me to heal. But, nevertheless, those who know me turn to me for some kind of help.

It saddens me if they think my only concern is to support them in their need; it seems such a waste of my healing love and power. But, as you know, I don't like to force myself on people. **If they ask for help, I give them help. If they ask for healing, I am ready to heal.**

77

Causes of Sickness

———— o ————

Consider my heart, child. Listen carefully. Where I see any of my children sick, I want to reach out to them in love. I want to speak the word to them which will set them free. I want to deal with the root cause of every sickness, not simply with the symptoms. The weed needs to be pulled out from the root. The situation often seems confused because the person is concerned with the symptoms and I am concerned with the cause.

Sometimes the cause is sin. Habitual sin has produced a pattern of sickness in the person's life. When sin is the cause, repentance brings amazing results.

Sometimes the cause is hereditary or genetic. I am able to free my children from such sickness. They certainly don't inherit illness from me.

Sometimes the cause is demonic. The enemy is a thief and he will steal physical health if he is able to do so. But I have overcome the power of the evil one. So, when my authority is brought to bear on the situation, the sickness has to depart.

Sometimes the cause is stress. Many of my people worry and grow anxious. This has a distressing effect on their bodies. Remember it is not only the physical disease which concerns, me, but what lies behind it. Repeatedly I tell my children not to fear, for this is a device of the enemy. He wants my children to be afraid because he knows the damaging effects of this on their health. I want my children to know my peace in spirit, soul and body. My Spirit can reach the depths of your being to free you from the negative pressures which have produced tension and disease.

My child, there are several other causes because each situation is unique. I deal with my children as individuals because my love for each is personal.

78

I Don't Want You to Be Sick

———— o ————

My dear child, understand that I never want you or any of my children to be sick. It is not my purpose for you – just as sin is not my purpose for you.

However, I allow you to sin and I can even use it in a positive way. I am able to redeem the situation and turn it to good in your life by drawing you to repentance and fresh obedience.

The fact that I am able to use sin by redeeming it does not make it my will for my children. The fact that sin often precedes a major spiritual breakthrough does not mean I want you to sin. Could the holy and righteous God ever want any of his children to sin? Of course not.

However, because of the weaknesses of those I have chosen, I know that inevitably they will sin. So I take this into account in determining how my purposes are to be worked out in each individual's life. When you sin, I don't disinherit you. It is the same with sickness, my child. **I don't want you to be sick,** but I know you can be. Just as you are prone to sin, so you are also prone to sickness.

I don't plan sin for you; neither do I plan sickness. I have to take account of both, however. I work within you in all circumstances for your good. Just as I do not disinherit you when you sin, so the fact you are sick makes no difference to your promised inheritance. I certainly don't condemn you for being sick. You can be sick as a Christian without incurring my disfavour; isn't that a relief? So don't live in any false fear of my disapproval. Rather, rejoice in my love, my care, my provision and healing.

Just as I can use a sinful situation to produce a major spiritual breakthrough, so I am able to use sickness in a refining, even in a creative way.

It is at this point that many misunderstand. Because **I am able to use sickness positively**, they assume that it must have been my will. They even suggest that I caused it deliberately in order to teach my child a lesson. Such an idea is an offence to my love. **Tell people that I am the Lord who heals.**

79

The Sick Woman

———— o ————

The woman lay on her sick-bed. 'I've been here so long,' she thought to herself. 'Doesn't anybody really care?'

She appreciated the friends who brought the flowers and the chocolates, and the cards from those who remembered her.

'But do they really care?' she asked herself. She welcomed those who came and prayed with her; they were so well-meaning and wanted the best for her. 'They seem to care,' she thought.

Then one night she saw her Lord in a dream. 'I care,' he said. When she woke, she left her bed of sickness.

80

Jesus Healed

———— o ————

When I became man in Jesus I clearly demonstrated what I thought of sickness by healing all who came to him with faith, and several others besides. When people came to him, he didn't send them away sick, telling them that I was using the situation to refine them, or that it was for their own good. He didn't tell them I was punishing them for their sins. He didn't say they must learn to live with their sickness.

No, **he healed them**. Yes, everyone who turned to him. He did this because he knew this to be my will. He would never go against my will in anything.

And when he went to the cross he dealt with every expression of evil, including sickness. Do you not perceive, my dear child, that I have created human beings with a desire to be well? They only function fully when they are fit.

81

Sickness is Distressing

———— o ————

I can understand that you often feel perplexed about the amount of suffering and sickness that exists in the world. And I know how distressing it is when someone close to you is ill.

Can you imagine how distressing it is to me? Yes, my child, I am deeply disturbed to see those I love in pain, whether emotional, spiritual or physical. My heart is full of love and compassion for the chronically sick, those who are disabled, deformed or mentally ill. I want to reach them with my love; I want to heal and bring peace to their souls and bodies. **It is my will to make them whole.**

If I want to heal, why do so many remain sick? I often have to settle for something less than my best in the lives of my children. I make the most of every situation. I am ready to give, to heal or deliver. I await the right opportunity.

My dear child, nothing makes you more perplexed than being ill. As soon as there is anything physically wrong with you, even a minor stomach ailment, you instinctively know that this is not my purpose for you and you have a great desire to be well again.

I want you to be strong and healthy. I am glad you are learning to resist sickness. When you feel the first symptoms, stand against them. Rebuke them in the name of Jesus. Don't imagine that you have to yield to the sickness.

Everyone needs healing in some way, for no one is perfect. But there are times when particular sicknesses attack and afflict you, making it difficult for you to do what I want. So, of course, I want to restore you. **I am glorified whenever I heal you.**

Some people think I can be glorified in sickness but this is not strictly true. I can be glorified in any of my *children* who are sick, but I am not glorified in the sickness itself. I regard sickness as something evil. You are not expecting to find sickness in heaven, are you? And Jesus has taught you to pray that my Kingdom shall come and my will shall be done on earth as it is in heaven. So of course I want to see people healed.

82

Receive Your Healing

———— o ————

Sometimes you have been afraid to ask me to heal you in case it doesn't happen. This is a trick of the enemy, isn't it? Fear is his weapon, not mine.

Sometimes you have asked only tentatively, hardly daring to believe I would answer. At other times you have grown stronger much more rapidly than you would have expected. On occasions when you need a miracle, I want to give you the faith to believe me for your healing. Nothing is impossible for me, child. You are beginning to believe this for your own life, aren't you?

There is no such thing as an incurable disease as far as I am concerned. **I am able to heal any sickness**. Human fathers and mothers want to help their children; they don't like watching them suffer pain, sickness or fever. This is even more true about me. I hate to see disease in your body. I am always at hand, child. I am listening to your prayer.

But, remember it is not your words that count but what you believe in your heart.

There have been times when it has not been right for me to heal immediately because there have been other things I have needed to sort out in you, especially when there are some relationships that aren't right. It is my policy to wait until you have forgiven; then I can release my healing power within you.

The secret of receiving healing is to believe that I love you so much that I want to give to you. It is a work of my grace. It helps, doesn't it, when you receive a specific word from me, for this encourages faith.

I heal directly and also through others. It is a wonderful thing when you know that your Creator has touched your life and healed you. It doesn't matter much what method I use, does it? It is the sheer wonder of knowing that you have received from me.

You know I am able to heal, and now you believe I am willing to do so. **When you pray, give me time to answer.** Don't be content with a quick prayer and then go rushing back to your activity. My hand is poised ready to bless but you need time to receive the blessing. I have so much to give, and so few give themselves time to receive. Remember, I don't heal only through instantaneous miracles but also through a continual process which I work out in your life.

83

I Hate Sickness

———— o ————

Tell me child, how do you feel about all those sick people who don't receive healing? Doesn't your heart go out to them? Don't you feel love and compassion for them? Well, this is how I feel too. But my love and compassion for them are far greater than yours. You question why more don't receive healing, especially those who appear to be my devoted followers. I know it perplexes you but I can assure you, child, that I am the only one who sees all the factors involved. Every decision I make is just.

I hate sickness and I would not wish it on any of my children. There are times when I use sickness as judgment on rebellious, stiff-necked, disobedient people. My word is clear about this, but it is certainly not my purpose for those who love me.

Sickness is a work of the devil but my power is so much greater than his. I allow the devil a certain amount of scope, but he never has the victory – not in the lives of any of my children. Death for my children is a release from pain and suffering. It is a release into my glory. **I always have the ultimate victory.** Each of my children is destined to have a new resurrection body which will not waste away.

84

I Was There in the Nightmare

———— o ————

My child, I was there in the middle of the nightmare – that period of your life when everything seemed to go wrong. Wherever you turned there were problems. Despair gripped you, didn't it? You felt as if you were entirely lost.

I was there when you even contemplated suicide. It was I who stayed your hand, for I would not want you to destroy yourself, so great is my love for you.

This was the most difficult time of your life, wasn't it? But you came through, my child, because I was there with you in the middle of it all. When you pass through the waters, I have promised they will not overwhelm you. When you go through the fire, you will not be burned.

I know how deeply hurt you felt at the time. You were experiencing a desolation such as Jesus experienced for you on the cross when he cried out, 'My God, my God, why have you forsaken me?' You felt forsaken, didn't you? Yet I was there all the time. I never left you.

I know the hurts that were inflicted upon you by others. I know also that those to whom you turned could not understand your dilemma. You see, they had never been where you had been. It seemed you were at the bottom of a great pit and nobody knew how to lift you out. But I came, didn't I? **I heard you cry. I came and rescued you and lifted you up.** I held you in my loving arms. I saw the joy slowly beginning to come back into your heart. I saw the peace gradually filling your soul; and I rejoiced.

It took some time, didn't it? But did you notice the point at which everything began to change? It was when you forgave. I watched you sink down a spiritual well, and resentment ate at your heart. You felt you had been dealt with so unjustly; one injustice seemed to be heaped on another. People turned against you and insulted you.

You cried out to me for vengeance. That is not what I tell you 'to do. **Forgive, love your enemies and pray for those who persecute you.** I had to wait until you were obedient to my word. I kept you through those difficult months until you began to rejoice in me and give thanks, even in those dire circumstances. Then everything began to change, didn't it? Have you learned the lesson well, my child?

In future, when others oppose and hurt you, will you let a root of bitterness spring up? Or will you be merciful and forgive? Instead of crying out to me in a rage of self-righteousness, will you praise me, knowing that I am the God of justice and that I vindicate my chosen ones?

I honour the truth and those who hold fast to my word. In my love, I cannot save you from the battles that lie ahead of you; but **I shall always be at your side and my Spirit will work within you for your good**.

85

The Battle Belongs to Me

———— o ————

I am like a mighty warrior who stands at your side with sword unsheathed to protect you from harm. The battle belongs to me. **You are more than a conqueror because of your faith in me**. But you have to live in my word to experience my victory.

I am a wall of protection around you, my child. When you walk in my way you are not vulnerable to the enemy. Even those who assault you, because they allow themselves to be instruments in his hands, will not cause you harm when you stand against them in the truth of my word.

My dear child, I have lifted you out of darkness and deep despair. Never sink back into that again. There is no need for that if you do as I say. Stand against every lie of the evil one. Don't entertain any of his thoughts. Don't believe any of his accusations. Don't accept any condemnation from him. I never want to see you sink into a pit of despair again. And you don't want to either, do you?

So, my child, walk before me in righteousness and in all the good things I have prepared for you. **Rejoice in me and let forgiveness and mercy flow from you as expressions of my love, even towards your enemies.**

86

I Am Light

———— o ————

My dear child, I am light. In me there is no darkness at all. I love to cause my light to shine where there is darkness. Every time this happens, the darkness has to disappear. You have noticed this in your own life, haven't you?

You see, I am engaged in a programme of bringing my light into areas of your life where still there is darkness, or at least shadows. Shadows of fear, unbelief, self-concern and defeat. I shine my light and those shadows disappear.

Sometimes you try to shield yourself from my light. That is never a clever thing to do because it prevents the liberation I want to bring to you. I always have my way in the end, don't I? But you are able to put off the day of your liberation through your hesitation.

I have made you a child of my Kingdom of light. So, walk in the light. Have nothing to do with the sinful deeds of darkness. Be constantly thankful that I have saved you from the corruption of this evil world.

Be one of my instruments in bringing light to those who live in darkness.

87

Powers of Darkness

——— ○ ———

The world is spiritually dark; evil forces are at work. These powers of darkness grip the lives of multitudes of people without their realising. They experience constant confusion, antagonism, sickness and despair as a result. They are in complete bondage in their social and moral lives, bound by these evil forces.

You see, my child, sin encourages darkness. Those who persist in their sins discover they cannot break free from them. They are enslaved. You can be thankful that I have saved you from such bondage.

I know your heart-concern for those who remain in darkness. All over the world I have raised up evangelists to bring them the light of my gospel. How distressing it is that so many hear the good news but are blinded by the god of this age. So they refuse to repent. They even make jokes about receiving the light! I long to see them turn to me so that **I can dispel their darkness with my light.**

88

I Dispel the Darkness

———— ○ ————

My dear child, there is a great spiritual battle happening all around you. It saddens me that so many Christians don't understand this. They are aware of the little conflicts within them, but don't believe in demonic powers although my word testifies to their reality. Jesus would not have rebuked demons if they did not exist. He would not have cast them out of people if they were not there in the first place.

People think that such powers belong only to primitive societies or to eastern nations. But I tell you that there are powers of darkness working all around you. They are invoked by those involved in black magic, witchcraft and the occult.

Often the devil appears as an angel of light. Those involved in spiritism imagine they do a great deal of good. But when they use other powers to heal, people are put in bondage to those powers. Calling on spirits of the departed is in direct contravention of my word. So I warn them to avoid every form of evil and be on the watch for deception. I never want to see people in bondage.

When I became man, my light came to live in the midst of the darkness of this world. All the powers of evil were hurled against Jesus but they could not prevail. On the cross, those dark forces were exposed and shattered.

I want you to understand the spiritual authority I have given you. I have made you a person of power and authority. Nothing is able to hinder you from walking in my ways. The powers of darkness cannot touch those who walk in the holy way of my light. They cannot pull them away from the light or drag them back into darkness.

No power of darkness need overcome you. I have given you, my child, authority over Satan and all his works. Whatever you bind on earth is bound in heaven. Whatever you loose on earth is loosed in heaven.

89

The Light of the World

—— o ——

Spiritual forces rule over areas, organisations and nations. They even try to infiltrate churches.

I hold you in my grip and will not allow anything to harm you. You are under the protection of the blood of the Lamb. The Holy Spirit who lives in you is greater than all the spirits of darkness that inhabit the world.

I am not suggesting that you go demon hunting, but you do need to be aware of their existence and the way they influence the society in which you live. They hold captive many whom you meet. Don't be surprised if demons try to attack you with oppression, heaviness or temptation.

You see, my child, I have put you in the front line. Sometimes you don't want to be there; you would much prefer to be among the reserve troops. But there are no reserve troops in my army! Every one of my children must be in the front line. Every believer is bound to be the object of attack from the enemy.

The best method of defence is attack. You are able to attack the enemy in your life and the lives of others. You have authority to set others free. You can command the enemy to depart from their lives as well as your own.

Before you gave your life to me you belonged to the kingdom of darkness. Jesus taught that Satan was your father. The enemy doesn't need to attack those who are already his! Some people even think it is better not to belong to me if they are going to be attacked. But I have delivered you from the dominion of darkness and brought you into my light.

You are no longer under the curse of Satan. My children are the light of the world. So **you are an ambassador of light**, child. This light has to be put on a table – not under it. I want your light to shine before men. Then they will see your good works and give me glory.

Don't be content because you have been delivered from the darkness; take my light where it is needed so that others too may be set free. Whenever you go in my name, I go with you. I watch over you; I care for you. I uphold you with my victorious right hand.

90

Live in Freedom

—— o ——

Often my children concern themselves with petty affairs while a spiritual war is taking place around them. They feel defeated by their circumstances because they are unaware of the true nature of the battle in which they are involved.

I want them to rise up in faith to exercise the authority and power I have given them. I have set my children free from the enemy; but some speak as if they are still bound.

It is for freedom that I have set you free. If I have set you free, you are free indeed. Walk in liberty as a child of God. Live free from the chaos and confusion caused by the evil one. Don't be afraid to come against him when you pray.

Submit yourself to me, resist the devil and he will flee from you. Would I tell you to do this in my word if it was not necessary? It is indeed necessary, my child. When he tries to plant negatives in your mind, resist those thoughts immediately. Don't receive them. If you allow him to affect your thinking, he can undermine your faith. Don't let him do this, my child. Listen to my word, not his lies.

You are not powerless to resist him, neither do you need to be afraid of him. He wants you to believe that if you resist him he will hit back in worse ways.

Your life is not to be lived under a cloud of such fear. I have called you to be a child of faith and to have confidence in me. This is my sovereign will for you.

91

My Sovereign Will

———— o ————

My dear child, people suggest everything that happens is my sovereign will. How they misuse this phrase.

Jesus demonstrated my sovereign will. He showed that I am merciful, that I forgive, heal and deliver my people. Sin, sickness and darkness are not my sovereign will. My will is that you live in me and I in you; that you obey me and live in the wonderful inheritance I have provided for you. **On the cross Jesus was oppressed to free you from all oppression, rejection and sickness.**

By contrast, the enemy wants you to feel ashamed, fearful and of no account. He says you are hopeless, worthless and useless. He discourages you with negative lies. I encourage you with the positive truth.

I am able to use you, and I'm going to do so for my praise and glory. My dear child, don't accept everything that happens as my sovereign will. You will only discover my will from my word. Don't live in fear: live in faith.

92

The Enemy's Tactics

———— o ————

My dear child, I want to explain to you some of the tactics of the enemy. The fruits of his labours are obvious. Wherever there is hatred, fear, destruction, violence, division, abuse, immorality, deception, deceit, corruption or lying, he has been at work. Just as I work through men, so he works through men. Just as I have available to me many angelic forces, so he works through demonic forces.

To look at the state of the world, you would think that Satan had the upper hand, for there is so much that is sinful and destructive. By comparison there seem so few who truly exalt my name. But you know well, my child, that the enemy does not have the upper hand.

Whenever light shines in the darkness, the light always prevails. **Satan is a defeated enemy.** The things you see happening in the world now are his last fling before he is thrown into the abyss for eternity. It is hardly surprising, therefore, that you should encounter opposition from him. He knows that you are on my side. He is like a trapped animal in its death throes, trying to reap as much destruction as possible before his ultimate end. But he shall not have you; you are mine.

He will attack you and seek to seduce you away from my purposes. He will try to deceive you by contradicting my word. He will tempt you to follow your course instead of mine. He will lie to you and accuse you in order to try to destroy your confidence. He will use others to criticise you so that you feel a failure and unworthy to be used in my purposes.

You will need to be alert to all his devices, child.

He seeks to sift you like wheat, but my Son has prayed for you. He intercedes for you in heaven continually. He prays for all who are his. I hear him and I honour his prayer for you.

93

Victory

———— o ————

I commanded the disciples to heal the sick and drive out demons. What I commanded those first disciples, I command you. Bring my victory into your circumstances and also the lives of others.

Beloved child, **I have defeated the evil one, and so have you.** He is crushed beneath my feet, and yours. Your faith has overcome the world and all the powers of darkness that seek to influence the world. You are no longer subject to them because you are subject to me. I am your Lord; Satan isn't.

I give angels to guard you at all times and my powers of light are infinitely greater than the powers of darkness. Walk in the light as a child of the light, rejoicing that your victory is assured.

All the powers of darkness are under judgment. So are those who invoke them. My judgment shall surely come upon them at the proper time, unless they repent. They will know my divine wrath for they honour the one who seeks to destroy the lives of those I have created.

I have spoken many words of love to you. You wonder whether this could be the same God who speaks of wrath and judgment. Well, it is still I who speak, my child.

You are not a child of wrath. You are a child of God. You are not under judgment and condemnation for my Son has saved you. You are no longer in darkness; now you live in light. You don't belong to the enemy camp. So don't apply to yourself words of judgment reserved for those who follow the enemy.

94

I Am Your Shield

———— o ————

I **am your Deliverer. I am your Stronghold. I am your**
Defence. I am a mighty Shield about you, my child. I
hold you in my arms of protective love. My gentle hands
are also strong hands, able to support you in the midst of
the battle.

Be alert and on the watch. The devil prowls around like
a lion seeking someone to devour. He will try to attack
you, but do not allow him to take advantage of you.

I care for those of my children who do not engage in
spiritual warfare. But they don't enjoy my full liberty.
They often walk under clouds of heaviness. They become oppressed and take tablets instead of exercising
their spiritual authority over those who oppress them.

Fear is one of his chief weapons; but you are not a child
of fear. I have not given you a Spirit of fear but of power,
love and a sound mind. My Holy Spirit is greater than all
the powers of darkness put together. He will lead you in
victory, so listen to him.

95

I Hate Darkness

———— o ————

My dear child, there are many who are gripped by foolishness. They don't want to invoke spiritual forces of wickedness. They don't want anything to do with the devil and yet they are involved with works of darkness: the occult, clairvoyance, palmistry, divining and horoscopes. There are organisations which appear to be instruments of light and yet lead people into bondage through secret rites of initiations. They invoke powers of darkness without understanding what they are doing.

Demonic powers work through witchcraft, orgies, drunkenness and satanic rites. But they can also influence people through drugs and consorting with prostitutes. Those involved in such things wonder why their lives are in such turmoil.

Some create and sell children's games which lead young minds into a prison of occult bondage. My righteous judgment is upon those who perpetrate such evil.

I weep over some of my children who smile about such things as if they were not of any significance. They are ignorant and deceived. **What a great task we have, child, to take my truth where there is such deception, to take my heart where there is such darkness. You are a child of my light.** Walk in the light; spread light.

96

Fight the Good Fight

—— ○ ——

My dear child, I want the devil to be exposed for who he is. He is the deceiver and accuser. He blinds people to spiritual truth. He is the father of lies. The deceit and deception that exist, the corruption that is everywhere in society, are the work of his hands.

He can rightly accuse those who belong to his camp, but not those who belong to my Kingdom. I save them from his accusations.

He is the thief who comes to steal, kill and destroy, even though he may appear as an angel of light. Praise me for giving you victory. I will teach you to fight the good fight of faith, confident that you are able to overcome every device of the evil one. You don't stand in the fight alone. But you are part of a mighty army I am raising up. And I am with you!

People wonder why I allow such powers to influence my world. I have already explained that those who have the ability to love must also have the power to hate. If they are able to walk in the light by choice, they must also be able to walk in darkness. For people to have a genuine choice to love and serve me, they must also be given the choice to serve the enemy.

I don't promise that life in this world will be easy. There will be tribulation, trouble and strife. I cannot save any of my children from being in the front line of the spiritual battle. **It is better to be engaged in the fight than to yield yourself to the powers of darkness.** These are the only alternatives.

Those who try to stand on some middle ground find that it doesn't exist! The enemy is able to rejoice over them and have victories in their lives, again and again.

Stand firm against the enemy. See him flee from you. Refuse to accept the lying, condemning, accusing thoughts, even when he voices these through other people around you. Refuse to compromise your walk in righteousness, holiness and truth. Refuse to have anything to do with the deeds of darkness.

These are important lessons I am teaching you, my dear child. At times you will not succeed. It will seem that the enemy has been allowed to gain the upper hand. Don't despair when this happens. I don't condemn you for your failure.

The evil one is jealous of you. For him there is no forgiveness; he is condemned to ultimate failure. But I forgive you and restore you to my victory. You are a child of light and the powers of darkness have no rightful claim on you.

You see, my child, I have won the victory, and you are able to establish that victory in the circumstances of your life as you exercise the authority I have given you. Persevere in faith until you see my victory.

As you walk in my light, you will rejoice. There will be singing and praises on your lips, for praise is the language of victory. In the middle of the conflict, keep your eyes on Jesus, the conqueror. **You are more than a conqueror through Jesus.**

97

I Am the God of Justice

———— o ————

My dear child, I am the God of justice. **I love justice and hate oppression,** which is a work of the enemy. I hate it when I see men oppressing others, and I love to see my children being liberated from oppression.

When my Son became flesh, he had to suffer oppression to liberate you from the oppressor.

I want you to understand, my child, how I view the nations. Because people see so much injustice, some think I created the world and then left it to its own devices. But no, my child, I oversaw the events of history. I cause nations to be raised up and I pull them down. I can use governments to execute my justice against other nations. Does this seem harsh to you? I never deal with anyone unfairly.

Because I love justice, what am I to do with whole nations who prefer sin and iniquity to righteousness? What am I to do with those who laugh at my name and oppose my purposes? What am I to do with those who exalt their false gods who can give no salvation or eternal life?

Some would like me to smile benignly on everybody. If I did that, I would deny myself. I would say that sin and wickedness didn't matter, that rebellion and blasphemy are not important, and that it doesn't matter which god you serve. All these things are so far from the truth.

I continue to hold out my hand in love, but I cannot force anyone to take it.

98

It Is Finished

——— o ———

My judgment is right, whether it involves nations, peoples or individuals. If I had not provided a sacrifice for sin, all would be consigned to death and eternal separation from me. That is the inevitable consequence of sin. But my justice is tempered with mercy. I don't want to condemn anyone. This is why I have reached out to my people through Jesus.

But what of those who spurn the blood of Jesus? What of those who deny he is my Son? What of those who prefer their own way instead of mine? They will receive the justice their deeds deserve. This saddens me, but I cannot act unjustly. I can't say that sin does not deserve its consequences. I have provided a way of escape from corruption. Can you blame *me* if people refuse my offer?

It saddens me when justice has to be executed in this way. Men reap the consequences of their sins.

Make my salvation known. I don't want to condemn; I want to save. I don't want to judge; I want to be merciful. But my mercy would not be necessary if judgment was not impending.

So many are taken up with their own fears. They are so wrapped up with themselves that they care nothing for the life I am offering them. This grieves me deeply.

Those who need my Son blaspheme him. Those who are in the depths of despair deny him. What more can I do? I can't force anyone to love me, for that would not be true love. I can't send another Saviour for Jesus has already done everything necessary for the salvation of mankind.

If they rejected him, do you really believe they would accept another? No matter at what time or period of history my Son came, he would have been welcomed in exactly the same way. A minority embraced him; the majority rejected him. The world denied him; the religious disowned him.

What has been done has been done. 'It is finished!'

99

My Righteous Judgment

———— o ————

My dear child, I know you are concerned about my righteous judgment on others. You fear for those who have rebelled and turned away from me. You are right to do so. But understand that **I don't enjoy judging anyone.** I don't joyfully test the hearts of those who are unfaithful. But I do rejoice over the faithful ones.

Through my forgiveness I have saved you from the righteous judgment you deserved. But what of those who do not know my forgiveness?

Many unsaved people ask that question. They want a god who will save everyone but make no demands on them. What deception! They don't want to face up to my righteous demands on their lives. So they say they don't believe in me. But who do they cry to when in need?

They don't want to believe in a God of righteousness. If they were to acknowledge me as such, they would have to change their attitudes and actions. They are not prepared to do this. It is easier to believe their own ideas about me instead of the truth. I show my anger from heaven against all sinful, evil men who push away the truth. When they give me up, I give them up to every evil practice they could think of.

Before a person can be forgiven, he must acknowledge his unrighteousness. There is no point in pretending he is right. He has to admit the truth. Those who reject righteousness reject eternal life. This grieves me because, in my love, I want my best for everyone.

100

I Love Everyone

———— o ————

My dear child, people often wonder how I regard those of other religions. They say, 'What about the Muslims, the Buddhists and Hindus, the Mormons and Jehovah's Witnesses? What about those who belong to eastern mystical cults?' Well, first it must be understood that I love them, because I love all men.

Who can think his way to heaven? Who can think his way into my presence? The eastern mystics deceive many by making it appear that this is possible. They suggest that knowing divine reality is an exercise of the mind. This isn't true, is it? It is only through my Spirit that divine truth can be imparted. You receive not only understanding, but life itself.

I know many are sincere, but I am sad that they are also deceived. They imagine they follow the truth when they don't. I am not afraid of competition, you understand! Nobody can compete with me.

But it is so futile, isn't it, that great multitudes of people can be so sincere and not know the forgiveness, mercy and compassion that you have experienced. It is sad, isn't it, that they can't receive the life you have received; life in all its fullness.

It grieves me that they don't receive my Spirit or the salvation I offer through Jesus. It saddens me to see that despite all their religiosity, they are still bound by their sin and guilt.

All I can do is reach out to them through my servants and reveal the truth to them. What am I expected to do if they deny the truth and the offer of life I give? There is nothing so blind as religious prejudice and deception.

People wonder how I will judge them. What is there to judge? They have chosen their gods. They look to them for salvation. How great is their misery if their gods are false. Pray for them, child. I love them.

101

My Covenant People

———— o ————

What of the Jews, my child? I am their God. It was to them that I came with salvation. They had the opportunity to be my instruments of salvation to the world, and for a generation they were just that. For it was through Jewish people that I first took my gospel to the nations. But the obedience of a few in one generation does not save all in other generations.

Rejection of my Son causes me great grief, for these are a covenant people to whom I have bound myself in faithfulness and love. Yes, my child, I truly love my Jewish people. But no one is saved through the law or any righteousness of his own. It is only through faith that a person can find acceptance in my sight and receive my gift of eternal life. This is true for Jew and Gentile alike.

You, my child, are an inheritor of the promises of both the old and new covenant because you have put your faith in Jesus.

Pray for my people the Jews. I have promised that when the Gentile nations have been gathered into my Kingdom then my Spirit will move among them and they shall accept Jesus as their Messiah. I rejoice over everyone who already acknowledges him as such.

I can see the time when there will be a glorious move of repentance and multitudes shall then accept Jesus as the

Christ. My Gospel will be preached to every nation before I come again. There will be a sovereign move of my Spirit among every people and in every land. I can see the end from the beginning, and I can see the harvest of Jewish souls that will be reaped before the end of time. I am he who keeps his word.

102

The Son and I Are One

———— ◦ ————

THOSE WHO BELIEVE IN JESUS BELIEVE IN ME.

THOSE WHO DISBELIEVE JESUS DISBELIEVE ME.

THOSE WHO LOVE JESUS LOVE ME.

THOSE WHO HATE JESUS HATE ME.

THOSE WHO OBEY JESUS OBEY ME.

THOSE WHO DISOBEY JESUS DISOBEY ME.

I AND JESUS ARE ONE.

103

Judging Others

—— o ——

My dear child, I alone decide those to whom I show mercy. Many are perplexed, wondering why only some are saved.

I don't judge by external appearances, but by the heart. Even when people rebel against me, I can see what will happen to them when they turn to me. I don't reach out only to those who appear to be good people. I reach out to the lost, forsaken, destitute, poor, and those who are bound by sin and walk in spiritual darkness. **I will go anywhere to save those who will be saved.**

Deception is the chief enemy of the truth. People imagine they are right but actually they believe lies. Satan is the father of lies, a liar from the beginning. All who deny the truth of Jesus have the devil as their father. Jesus made that clear. But they are accepted by me when they turn to me, asking for forgiveness and surrendering their lives to me.

No one can be saved in his sins but only from them.

What becomes of those who have never heard of Jesus and don't understand the gospel? I shall give every man justice. I will never deal unfairly with anyone. It is not for you to know what will become of them. You are not the judge of anyone else.

Don't seek to understand things that are too hard for you. I give you knowledge and revelation, but there are some things which are not yours to know. Your eternal destiny is assured, but **I would never give you knowledge which would make you the judge of others.** I would not make you God. Even Jesus in his humanity didn't come to judge. Why then should you be a judge? Isn't it better to leave all judgment to me? Receiving my life does not make you a judge of anyone else, but rather a servant of all. Seek to live in my love and reach out with my truth. This is all I want, dearest one.

104

The Forgiven

———— o ————

'They get what they deserve, those brutes. They don't care about anybody else. They're only interested in themselves. If I had my way, they would all be locked up.'

'Bring back the rod,' his friend replied.

'Why not hang the worst of them?' another said. 'Let's rid the earth of them.'

Another sat quietly in the corner and thought to himself, 'I used to be one of them: violent, selfish, a thief and a liar. But he saved me.'

105

Hell

———— o ————

My dear child, you know me in my love, gentleness and tenderness. You have been spared the harsh reality of my judgments. To keep heaven holy, I had to condemn the devil and his angels to hell. They are held for final judgment.

When I could see righteousness in no one except Noah, I caused the flood as my judgment upon an unbelieving and godless generation. At other times, cities have been wiped out in judgment. Nations have been destroyed and overcome because they chose to follow tyrants instead of me. Make no mistake, my child: **judgment upon the unholy is harsh, even though it is fairly and righteously administered.** The wages of sin are death and eternal separation from me. When I express my wrath in judgment it is never because I have lost my temper. Every judgment I make is a calculated act of justice, having given opportunity for people to respond to my truth.

Hell is a reality. Can you imagine eternal separation from me? Can you envisage what is meant by wailing and grinding of teeth, or being consigned to outer darkness? You cannot imagine these things because you are a child of the light. But I can see the awful reality of what awaits the lost. I don't want my people to be robbed of the eternal destiny I have chosen for them. All have sinned and fall short of my glory but **eternal life is my free gift to all who turn to me.**

106

Men Form Their Own Judgment

———— o ————

Consider the rulers of the nations. Many of them are more concerned with power than the welfare of their people. They are more concerned with their own kingdoms than my heavenly Kingdom. Most care little or nothing for me. What am I to do with them if they avoid the opportunity to bless my people and work for their own welfare instead? What about ordinary people? Are they simply ignorant and blinded? Have they chosen to serve the one who offers worldly riches, position and happiness?

I offer all the riches and resources of my Kingdom. I offer true joy. Some taste my riches but then see the cost of discipleship. They turn back to their own ways and deny me. I grieve for them especially. I long for their return. Many do come back but some are lost for ever. What grief it causes me that men should see the light and yet choose the darkness. This is why I say to you, my child, walk in the light as a child of the light.

My people can choose blessing or curse, life or death. Of course, I want them to choose blessing and life because I love them. But the choice is theirs.

Many misunderstand judgment. They imagine I sit on a throne and make on-the-spot decisions as to what I should do with each person when he dies. I don't have to make any such decisions. People have already made their own, haven't they? They face the inevitable consequences of their decisions.

Each man will receive the just reward for what he has done. Those who have chosen the way of salvation shall surely be saved; but those who have denied Jesus as the only way of salvation shall inevitably be lost.

107

The Narrow Way

———— o ————

Those who judge me don't know my ways, neither do they understand my love. They don't see the heaviness in my heart, or the anger I feel towards the perpetrators of evil who cause death and destruction to my people. Do I not have the right to show fury and power against those who are fit for destruction?

I have my witnesses in every nation. Where there is persecution my people thrive and my Kingdom is extended. Persecution encourages people to be more dependent on me.

Is martyrdom really necessary? Yes! The blood of martyrs is never spilt in vain. Their blood shall be avenged in due course. **Those who oppose my people oppose me.** Don't you know my heaviness of heart concerning all who reject me?

Those who know me are so concerned with the plight of others that they use every opportunity to speak of my salvation. They devote their lives to the cause of my Kingdom.

Religious people are supposed to be enlightened, aren't they, child? Yet still many of them choose to believe what they want to believe, instead of my word. Oh, my child, don't you realise how shameful it is for anyone to confess the name of Jesus and yet side with the perpetrators of evil? They create their own way of following me because they don't like the true way. They confess the name of Jesus, yet choose the broad way that leads to destruction instead of the narrow way that leads to life.

108

Not Under Wrath

—— o ——

I rejoice over you because you remain faithful to me. I am pleased with you and delight in you. You long for me, don't you: to know me better, to be closer to me, to be used effectively by me?

The devil tries to encourage you to believe I am displeased with you, that you are a disappointment to me. But don't you see now, my child, that **my disappointment lies elsewhere. I don't disapprove of you,** but of those who reject my Son. They are the objects of my wrath, not you.

Thank you for accepting me. Thank you for loving me. Thank you for following me. You shall receive your due reward. Thank you, dearest child.

109

I Am the Truth

———— o ————

My dear child, I am the Truth. Yes, truth is a person, not a set of ideals! I am not like the enemy who deceives, or like men who are unreliable. I am light and in me there is no darkness. I don't need to deceive because I am not ashamed of any of my actions.

I have come to the world as the word, Jesus. He came full of grace and truth. He expressed my truth in everything he said and did. He exposed the works of the deceiver. He broke the hold of spiritual darkness over people's lives. He spoke words of truth which set people free – from past bondages, from the grip of evil, from sin and despair, from sickness and need. He set them free to love and serve in ways which are pleasing to me.

Sin is deceptive. When you sin, my child, you feel awkward in my presence, or you want to avoid me altogether. You hope your sin doesn't become exposed. **But when you walk in the truth, you have nothing to hide from me or from anyone else.** You experience the freedom I intend for my children.

Sometimes I have to confront you with the truth of who I am, of my claims on your life, or with what you have done. Don't be surprised or discouraged by this. It is my way of bringing you to freedom.

110

The Truth Works

———— o ————

Can you see that truth works? It grieves me to see some pick and choose when they read my word. They will believe this, but not that. They will accept this, but not that. They will do this, and not that. They sit in judgment on the truth, often on the supernatural dimensions of my word. They forget I am supernatural and try to follow me by trusting their natural reason and ability, and then wonder why they flounder. They don't trust what I say, and then try to excuse themselves for their unbelief.

They suggest my words may not be reliable, that I am incapable of ensuring that only the truth is contained in scripture. In two thousand years of intellectual achievement, have people progressed beyond spiritual truth? During this period, have I lost some of my ability and dynamic power, that I no longer want to love my children by healing them and performing miracles? Have my purposes changed?

I have made clear that **my truth never changes;** heaven and earth will pass away but my words will not pass away.

What am I to do with such an unbelieving and perverse generation? What can I do, except patiently bide my time, and bless all those who hold to the truth of my word with an honest and good heart?

Still, it is good that you believe me, child. To believe I am the truth is to believe what I say. You have learned who is right when your reason and my word conflict!

Over the years I have patiently changed your mind over many issues – not by forcing you but by presenting you with the truth again and again.

You have found some of my promises difficult to accept because you keep looking at your experiences which seem to contradict what I say. If you look at my promises instead, your circumstances will change.

Don't fall into the trap of believing promises without accepting the conditions which go with them. This is a mistake which many make. **Listen carefully to everything I say to you.** Remember who is speaking. I am no mere man; I am your Lord and your God. When I speak it is with all my divine authority. It isn't that some things are more true than others. Truth is truth. Whether I am addressing major situations or giving revelation about details, all I say is the truth.

111

Don't Judge My Word

———— ◦ ————

Who will set himself above me to judge me? Who dares to judge the words of my Son, or to discredit what is written under the inspiration of my Spirit? Could it be that some value their opinions above my word? What pride! What arrogance!

What should I do with such people? They judge themselves by what they believe. If they value their own opinions and ideas, then only their opinions and ideas work for them. **But if they value the truth, the truth will work for them; and I am that truth.**

My dear child, listen to the truths my Spirit of truth impresses upon you. Don't push them away. My truth is the answer to every need. It sets you free!

112

Cling to the Truth

———— o ————

I am the Truth. Those who cling to me cling to my word. Instead of believing their feelings, they learn to believe what I say. They put their trust in me rather than in their circumstances. This is what I have been teaching you.

Trust my love, no matter how dark and depressing things may seem. Rejoice in me always, no matter what the circumstances. Maintain your peace even in the midst of turmoil and confusion. Knowing me as the truth will enable you to go through times of conflict and difficulty with triumph.

I have made you a new creation; that is the truth. I have set you free from the law of sin and death; that is the truth. I have come to live in you by the power of my Spirit. I have blessed you with every spiritual blessing in Christ. You are more than a conqueror as you put your trust in me. Constantly I remind you of the truth that nothing is able to separate you from my love. **All this is the truth about you!**

The truth can never be changed. What is true for you is true for each one of my children, whether an international evangelist or the newest believer. Each is precious in my sight. Each has the same inheritance. I don't discriminate between my children. I want all of them to enjoy all of me; and that is the truth! So I have given them everything they need for life and godliness.

You need to be reminded of these things from time to time, don't you, child? Sometimes you flow in the revelation of my truth, rejoicing in all I am and all I have done for you. But sometimes you slip out of gear. You take your eyes off the truth and place them on yourself. Then you begin to struggle.

This is not my purpose for you. **Keep your eyes on me and you will keep your eyes on the truth.** It sounds very simple, I know. But the reality is often more difficult, isn't it?

113

The Man With the Stoop

———— ○ ————

There was a man who carried a heavy load for many years. He felt weighed down by his problems. They were like a large pack on his back. So great was the weight that the burden caused him to stoop.

One day his burden was removed. He rejoiced that the weight had been lifted from his back. He knew he was set free from it. He knew that only the Lord could have lifted such a burden from him. But still he continued to stoop.

The Lord spoke to him: 'Stand up straight, son.' The man heard these words but in his heart he replied, 'I can't stand up straight. I will have this stoop for the rest of my life because of the burdens I have carried for so long.'

114

Feed on the Truth

———— o ————

The time you spend studying my word is so precious and important, for this is when you build your relationship with the truth. **The truth encourages you, doesn't it child?** I want it to be lodged in your heart.

115

The Walk

———— o ————

There was a man who set out on a very long walk. He knew the general direction in which he had to go but he had no map to guide him. Consequently he took many false turnings which made his journey still longer.

Then one day he came to a village and decided to ask someone which direction he should take. 'Have you no map?' he was asked.

'None,' he replied.

'Here, take this,' said the stranger, thrusting a book into his hand.

'What good is this to me?' said the man. 'When will I have time to read such a long book? I will trust in my own instincts to get me to my destination. Besides, I would only have to carry this book with me.'

And so he threw it aside. Will he ever reach his destination?

116

I Am Faithful

———— o ————

I don't have to explain my actions or justify myself before men. I am righteous, so I always act righteously. I am love, therefore I always act in love. **I am faithful and I always act faithfully.**

My dear child, you must understand that I never deny myself. I will never act contrary to my nature. I reveal myself in what I do.

I have always been faithful to you, even when you have been faithless. I have been utterly reliable and dependable. I have been with you always, loving you through every crisis, watching over you with tender care, even when you have been determined to pursue your own course and not mine. I have seen your impatience when I have not answered prayer in the way you wanted; and then later I have seen your relief that I didn't answer you in that way.

People judge me by the failure of my children. But I am never responsible for their sin. I am responsible for their pardon, forgiveness and restoration.

If I was as fickle as some people imagine, this would be a crazy world. There would be no order, only chaos. But I haven't only created by my word: I sustain creation by my word. If I was to be unfaithful to what I have said, the whole universe would go into confusion and chaos.

The reason why there is so much disorder in the world today is because many listen to the lies and deceit of the enemy, placing themselves under his control. He deceives: I am faithful. So I can truly say that heaven and earth will pass away, but my words will not pass away. I watch over them to ensure they are fulfilled.

117

You Want to Be Faithful

—— o ——

My dear child, I know that one of your deepest fears is that you will prove unfaithful to me. But if you keep trusting me, this will not happen. You see, **those who trust my word obey my word. Faithfulness is expressed in obedience.** Don't simply believe the promises, but take note of the commands as well. Glorify me in every aspect of your life.

The enemy tries to persuade you that you want to be unfaithful. Don't listen to him, even when he persists in his accusations. Don't feel you have to fulfil these lying thoughts, or be deceived into thinking this is your destiny.

These are pernicious lies. They have trapped many of my children, causing them to be involved in sin unnecessarily. Don't listen to such accusations. I have put into your heart a desire to please me in all things. Your lapses and failures don't amount to persistent sin, which comes from a rebellious heart. **You want to be faithful,** don't you? Who put that desire in your heart? I did. So I will ensure it is fulfilled because you are determined to walk in my ways.

Yes, my child, I need your co-operation. I know I will have that because you really want to please me. You build on rock when you build on me. You will be able to withstand every storm and difficulty. Nothing will cause your house to fall. **Honour my word at all times.** Those who build their house on the rock are those who hear my word and do it.

I am your Rock. I love to support you, no matter what the situation. I am like a firm foundation that cannot be moved. I'm not a tiny boulder but the bedrock of your life. I am your faithful Father who loves you and cares for you. I am your Provider and your Healer; you shall lack nothing, neither shall you be overcome. I am the Almighty One. Nothing is impossible for me.

118

Do You Believe?

—— o ——

How many believe I will honour the promises of my word? Some believe them for others, but not for themselves.

They know that I am almighty, all-powerful, and therefore nothing is impossible for me. But do they expect me to do the impossible in their own experience? I tell them they can ask me for anything in the name of Jesus, but do they believe me? Do they think I will be true to such words? Or do they imagine these to be empty promises, a strange spiritual language that bears little or no relation to reality?

Some complain that when they pray with what they imagine to be faith, they still do not see the answers they need. They question my integrity and truthfulness!

It is true that I choose to work in different ways from those they want. Most of my children like instant answers; they don't like to be kept waiting. They snap their prayer fingers and expect me to come running, but are they as responsive when I speak to them? They want me to be faithful without being faithful themselves.

I always answer the prayers of my children with wisdom. I never make mistakes, neither do I fail. Many rush around in a fever of activity, wondering why I don't give them the answers they need. They are neither patient, nor do they persevere in faith. I will answer but in my way, not theirs.

I am always faithful but I come in for much criticism over what they call 'unanswered prayer'. There is no such thing. **I never ignore the prayers of my children.** I don't shut my divine ears to their hearts, or my eyes to their need. I listen intently and always do what they believe I will do, just as I have promised.

Notice that I listen to their hearts. Many pray the right-sounding words but don't believe their own prayers. Am I expected to answer their words or their hearts? **I have promised to answer what they believe in their hearts and I am faithful in doing this.**

119

True Faithfulness

———— o ————

When people accuse me of unfaithfulness, they fail to notice that there may have been other factors which prevented them from receiving what I wanted to give. Some stop praying. So much for their perseverance and faith! Others say they only want me to answer if it is my will. I am certainly not going to give them what is opposed to my will! When people pray like this, they are not sure what they believe or expect.

Jesus teaches you to believe that you have received whatever you ask in prayer. Then it will certainly be yours!

Those with true faith trust me no matter what the circumstances. Even when they don't see an immediate transformation in the situation when they pray, they keep trusting, knowing that **I will fulfil every promise I have made.**

This is the kind of faithfulness that comes from my heart; it is the kind of faith I am producing in you. I like it when you believe my words and act upon them. This will make you really fruitful beyond anything you could have imagined.

Jesus was faithful to me throughout his ministry. You and I can have the same relationship of love and unity, grounded in faithfulness. I am encouraging you not only to believe in my faithfulness but to be faithful yourself.

Be faithful in living out my word. Reflect my faithfulness in your relationships. Don't allow your circumstances to change your love or commitment but maintain your faithfulness, laying down your life for your friends and loving as I have loved you.

Have you noticed that I have maintained my faithfulness to you, no matter what your response to me? Well, in this same way, maintain your faithfulness to others, no matter what their response to you. You will not always find it easy. Nevertheless, this is the only course open to you. Your faithfulness to others truly honours and glorifies me.

120

Trust Me

———— o ————

I am faithful to myself. I am faithful to my word. I am faithful to the blood of my Son. **And I am faithful to you**, my beloved child. The more you put your trust in me, the more you experience my faithfulness. Rejoice in this.

The more you trust my word, the more you will see my word fulfilled in your life. The more you trust in the work of the cross, the more you will live in freedom from guilt, shame, grief, sickness, fear and failure. My Spirit's presence within you is my guarantee that I really will give you all I have promised. The Spirit's seal upon you means I have already purchased you and guarantee to bring you to myself.

The more you trust in my love for you, the more you will enjoy life and know victory in trying circumstances.

I have promised to finish the good work I have begun in you. I will not leave you semi-sanctified! You will be fit for heaven because of all I have done for you and in you. So rejoice!

121

I Am Wisdom

———— o ————

My dear child, I am wisdom. **I always act wisely.** I never do anything foolish. I always speak words of wisdom, whether in scripture or by my Spirit.

I want to eradicate foolishness in you. I often hear you say, 'What a fool I've been'. You look back on things you have said or done and realise how foolish you have appeared to others. This causes you acute embarrassment. It seems worse when others think you are foolish, doesn't it? This confirms all your fears about yourself.

Sin is foolishness. Whatever opposes my will is foolishness. Yielding to temptation is foolishness. I don't condemn you for these things, as you are beginning to realise at last. But my Spirit working within you prompts you to be wise in every situation and on every occasion. So take note of what he says.

My wisdom is pure. So, avoid what is impure in my sight. Sometimes you don't want purity because sin can be fun, at least while it lasts. But when you know you have offended me, you feel dirty and are not clean again until you have repented and received my forgiveness. You don't like feeling dirty, do you? To be clean is to be at peace with me, with nothing to restrict or inhibit your joy.

Jesus made clear that to perform the sin in the mind is as bad as doing the deed itself. Don't misunderstand what he says or you will place yourself in false condemnation. Having the thought or the temptation that the enemy plants is not the sin, but dwelling upon it and making it a focus of desire. If you encourage the thought, it becomes a sinful fantasy.

So in your fight against sin, child, be wise. Dismiss anything impure or opposed to my word. You will be all the better for it. I want to spare you from unnecessary conflict. Remember that Jesus was tempted in every way just as you are, yet he was without sin; he always resisted. I never allow you to be tempted beyond what you are able to endure. I've made that clear to you before, haven't I?

122

Words of Wisdom

——— o ———

My dear child, it is wise to know my word, to be familiar with the truth. They are words of life and healing.

I want my word to be like a reservoir within you. You can draw on this living water in every situation. My Spirit will remind you of my truth. So it is unwise to be ignorant. You don't understand all you read in the Bible, but you understand enough to know what I want in most situations. When you need fresh wisdom or understanding, ask me and I will give it to you.

My Holy Spirit will always lead you in the path of wisdom. This means you will pursue the way of peace, gentleness and kindness – qualities which the world often despises as weakness. Well, they are qualities I possess and I am certainly not weak! I made the universe!

So if you display these same qualities, you will be able to make better use of the power I've given you.

When I reach out to you in the gentleness of my love, something powerful happens in your life, doesn't it? My Spirit works with gentleness, love and affection, and also brings power, deliverance and healing.

Is it your prayer always to act in wisdom? Others will be very quick to pounce on any area of foolishness in your life. **If you walk in wisdom, you will have nothing to fear** from them. You will make mistakes because everybody does. Others may laugh at you as a result, but I don't laugh at you. I encourage and forgive you.

123

This is Wisdom

———— o ————

My dear child, it is wise not only to hear the scriptures but to believe and live them, and do as I say. Believe me when I speak to you, saying that you are lovely in my sight, precious beyond compare. Believe me when I say you are the apple of my eye, that I have redeemed, called and saved you.

I am not a stern Father who remains at a distance, giving wise advice. I am your loving Father who draws near to you, embracing you in love. Walk with me in my ways of wisdom. Be wise as I am wise. Avoid the foolishness of sin and you will rejoice with great joy.

My wisdom leads to peace and is expressed in righteousness, holiness, integrity, truth, love and power. Can you see how all these things are related?

Fear of me is the beginning of wisdom. You are in awe of who I am, so avoid every form of evil and all that is opposed to my word. You are able to have wisdom beyond your years because of the way my Spirit flows through you. Don't despise experience for, although wisdom comes as a gift from me, you learn how to exercise that wisdom by experience. **Wisdom protects you from evil.** It also encourages humility. The foolish are arrogant; Jesus was both wise and humble.

Just as my Spirit of wisdom rested on Jesus, so my Spirit of wisdom rests on you. This is why you feel uneasy if you step outside my purposes. Do you remember that in his humanity, Jesus grew in wisdom? This is what is happening with you. You can only sit at my feet, hear and learn from me because my Spirit of wisdom is operating within you, bringing revelation. This is very different from worldly wisdom which passes away; my wisdom lasts for ever.

Don't think that wisdom is beyond you. You will have sufficient wisdom in every situation. It is time that you really thanked me, child, that I have given you wisdom. **You have my wisdom and can act wisely in every situation.**

124

My Authority

———— o ————

I have total authority over all creation, the whole universe. I have authority in heaven. I have authority over the devil; he only has leave to do what I allow in the testing of men's hearts.

I have complete authority over the nations. I am able to raise up and pull down governments. I can even bring nations into being and cause them to pass away.

I have authority over my Church and **I have authority over you** as one of my children.

My dear child, it is right to respect my Lordship, to be in awe of my majesty and glory, but don't be afraid of me. For although I possess all authority, it is not my purpose to demolish my children. Look how I have encouraged you.

Some people think I don't make a very good job of the exercise of my authority. They point to the conflicts among nations, to the corruption in governments, to the ineffectiveness of my Church and to the failure of some of my children. They judge and condemn me for these things, saying that if I am Lord, I should make a better job of my position!

Some leaders govern well; others oppress through their pride or corruption. Yet in the midst of all this I am at work hearing the heart-cries of my children, establishing righteousness through those who love me. While people are blaming me, I am at work in the situation, changing things!

125

My Critics

———— o ————

My critics want me to act more quickly to eradicate the suffering and need caused by men's corruption. What hypocrisy, for these very critics don't want to acknowledge my authority in their own lives. They don't want me to judge their hearts and actions, but won't repent of their sins. They don't want to bring their lives into conformity to my will or submit to my Lordship.

There is such suffering, injustice and corruption in the world because so many deny my sovereignty.

Some point to the desperate plight of the poor, holding on to their riches while they do so, enjoying their comfortable life-style. Others point to moral depravity while enjoying their own sins. They speak against corruption although their own affairs are not in my order. They complain about the amount of sickness, and yet serve the one who brings sickness, disease and devastation into the lives of people.

They complain about the way they are governed, but don't want to be governed by me. They don't believe my word and neither do they obey me. They criticise me in a futile attempt to justify their disobedience, unbelief and rebellion against my authority.

In my Church many acknowledge my authority only superficially. As a result, the Body of Christ is not the effective instrument in the world it should be. They call me 'Lord' without allowing me to be Lord in their lives.

If everybody who belonged to a church truly submitted their lives to my Lordship, there would be no divisions. Men would not fight with each other for power; they would not squabble, be angry or jealous of one another. Instead they would radiate the life of Jesus more fully and effectively.

126

My Authority in Jesus

———— o ————

My authority was seen in Jesus. He demonstrated my Lordship in the way he spoke and the actions he performed. He gave the command and the waves obeyed him, demons were driven out of people, the sick were healed. Even the dead were raised.

At the same time he recognised my authority over him. He submitted to my heavenly will, speaking only what I gave him to speak, doing only what he saw me do, obeying me even to the point of death. **He exercised my authority perfectly because he submitted to my authority perfectly.**

This would happen in my Church today if people were prepared to submit to my authority in the same way. But because there is so much disobedience, there is often little truly spiritual authority or evidence of my Lordship.

I cannot be head of rebellion, sin or disobedience. I am obviously not Lord in the life of someone who works in his own ways instead of submitting to mine, no matter how many times he goes to church or prays. Where there is genuine submission to my authority, there my Church appears strong and healthy. My Spirit is able to work powerfully through my people to liberate others.

127

My Authority in Your Life

———— o ————

My dear child, when you submit to my Lordship you are an effective witness and a fruitful member of the Body. I can use you to express my life. **You are able to speak and act with my authority.**

So, my child, recognise my authority in your life. This is not a matter of saying, 'Lord, Lord'. Some call me 'Lord' but will not enter my Kingdom because they don't do what I say. To submit to my authority is to submit to my word and my will.

Quietly, lovingly, but with great determination, I have been establishing my authority in your life. You are now in the middle of this process. You acknowledge me as your Lord, but still there are areas where you fail to submit to my authority.

In some ways you don't want to submit to me, do you? You wish I would compromise my demands upon you. You would like me to change my word to conform with your desires.

You know I won't do this, don't you? That would jeopardise the whole purpose I am working out in your life. Instead I change your heart, purify your desires and bring you more in line with my will and authority.

Sometimes I have to speak about a matter several times before you take notice of what I say. My dear child, this is evidence of the fact that you still have some way to go in understanding my authority.

Wouldn't it be wonderful if I only had to speak to you once and immediately you acted upon my word? You delight me on the occasions when this happens. It thrills my heart.

I wait for you to work through many desires and fears before you are ready to accept my will. There are times of conflict when you weigh one thing against another. Will you obey or disobey? Well, my child, I want you to know that I never give up. I continue lovingly, gently, but firmly to impress on you what I desire until you do come to a full acceptance of my will.

Sometimes you think you know better than I do! **But things only work out for the best when you are happy to submit to my authority.** It isn't very comfortable fighting against me, is it?

128

Submit Joyfully

———— o ————

Here's something else you need to understand. I want you to delight to do my will, even when it is not what you want. Doesn't this seem a contradiction? It is. Don't you think it would be much easier to submit at the beginning? This would save you from a load of anguish, anxiety and conflict. Only a suggestion, my dear child! I would love to save you from these inner conflicts in the future.

I know you only too well, and there will be further times of conflict. But I am encouraged by the fact that you are learning through experience. Peace is much better than conflict, isn't it? I want my peace to keep your heart and mind in the knowledge of my love for you.

I always exercise my Lordship in love. Whatever I command, I ask of you in love; I want you to respond in love. You are afraid that I will make demands of you beyond your abilities. You are afraid to draw too close to me because you fear you may lose the freedom to do what you want. But I have impressed on you many times that I will never interfere with your free will, no matter how close you draw to me or how well you know me. I will only work with your co-operation. If the demands seem great to you sometimes, this is only because I know you have reached the point where you are able to meet those demands.

I don't ask things of my children which are beyond them. I take into account that I make my supernatural power available to them. I will never crush my children by putting them in situations where they are trapped, and cannot possibly do what I say.

If you agree to walk in my ways you will not be afraid of my authority. You will be glad to do my will, exercising my authority in your own life and ministry, speaking, praying and acting in my name.

You will be able to speak with my authority to mountains of need and see them moved, to speak to diseases and see them healed. You will speak words of forgiveness to those who have been enslaved by guilt. People will see what you do and hear what you say and they will know that I am your Lord.

129

Authority in My Church

———— o ————

My dear child, I know that sometimes you are per-plexed about the way to relate to the authority of men, especially within my Church. It seems to you that it is one thing to recognise and acknowledge my personal authority over you, but it is quite another to have to submit to my authority in others. Yet I ask you to do this.

I want you to listen to me very carefully. **I don't place my children under the spiritual authority of those who are not equipped to exercise such authority.** This is the mistake some of my children make. They feel they have to submit to the authority of men in the places where they are, but these are not the places where I want them.

How can someone exercise spiritual authority in my name if they don't acknowledge my authority in their own lives? How can leaders have spiritual oversight of my people if they are not spiritually alive themselves? This seems so obvious. Why do many imagine they have to submit to unspiritual men in unspiritual churches?

Well, my child, I tell you plainly, that is not my way. I provide appropriate spiritual oversight for my children in order to see them raised in faith and love, and equip-ped for the ministry to which I call them. Those who submit to unspiritual leadership are not encouraged in their faith, nor in love; neither are they released in ministry. Instead they are suffocated by their circumstances.

My people have often tried to reduce my word to a series of legalistic formulae. Authoritarianism is of the flesh, not of my Spirit. It is men's substitute for the real thing. Spiritual authority comes not from a man's position in any church system, but from his standing with me. **He is only able to exercise authority through the anointing I place on his life.** Does this make things clearer to you?

There is to be great respect among my children for those who lead them. I want spiritual leaders to act in my name and declare my authority in the life of the whole body. How can my children respect the authority of those who are unspiritual? Yet so many of them remain in situations where they cannot respect authority because there is none to respect. This saddens me. I want to see my children growing and prospering in the things of my Spirit.

130

True Authority in Leaders

———— o ————

How it rejoices my heart when leaders exercise authority because they are so submitted to my authority themselves. Such leaders are not men pleasers! They don't simply follow the whims and fancies of any congregation. **They want to please me by leading my people in the way I want them to go.** Such leaders delight me.

Their task is not always easy. Within any fellowship there are those who don't want to submit to my authority. They don't truly want my Lordship over that fellowship. They want to run the church in their own way for their own ends, in order to see their own desires fulfilled. I weep when congregations are manipulated by such people. They cannot be a true expression of my Body.

I want leaders to be people of authority who will declare my purposes without compromise, leading my people unswervingly in the way I want them to go.

Submit to those who are in true authority over you. They will help, encourage and strengthen you in the things of my Spirit. But I don't ask you to submit to those who will hinder, discourage and frustrate you.

However, my child, don't expect perfection in your leaders. They are only human like you. I am working in their lives as I am working in yours – refining, purifying, causing them to increase in love, wisdom and faith.

Don't worry if on occasions they make mistakes. If the leadership consists of those who are truly led by my Spirit, they will soon be convicted of their mistakes and will not continue in pride, trying to maintain they are right on every occasion. They are humble and submit to me. They are humble before the people they lead. Authority is not seen in pride and arrogance but in gentleness, love and sensitivity to the voice of my Spirit.

If you look for perfection in leaders you will never be satisfied, no matter what fellowship you belong to. Learn to respect my authority and submit to one another.

131

I Give My Life

———— o ————

My dear child, no matter how much you have received from me, I still have so much more to give. I am bursting with life, longing to give. Isn't it sad that so many worship me but don't believe I want to give them anything? Yet it blesses me to give: I live to give myself to my children. So I delight when you turn to me to receive, when you are prepared to stop your busy schedule, sit down with me and receive from me. It delights me. This is what I want: to give and give and give to you.

Some people criticise those who want to receive constantly from me. The critics are usually the busy ones rushing around in a fever of activity. But I am wise. I know that the more I give my children of my abundant life, the more that life will flow through them to others. Yes, my child, this is why I want you to receive from me.

Don't be content to receive only occasionally and then try to keep going for a long time in the good of that blessing. **I want to give to you daily, several times a day, in whatever way is needed.**

I am generous by nature. You don't have to persuade me to give.

132

Receive the Holy Spirit

———— o ————

Every time one of my children asks to be filled with the life of my Holy Spirit, I always answer their prayer affirmatively. Some think they haven't received because they haven't trusted me to be faithful in honouring my promise. But I love to give my Holy Spirit to those who ask. Why serve me in your own strength?

I am weary of theological arguments. Some of my children argue about when and how to receive the Holy Spirit, whether a believer can receive only once or often. They argue and argue. Many of them don't come to me to discover the answer. If they did, they would discover I never come to the end of my giving.

If two people love each other, they keep giving to one another. If they ever stop giving, that is a sign that their love has grown cold. They may continue their relationship on a formal or legalistic basis, but they have lost the true spontaneity of love.

I love to give my life to my children at any time, in any place, on any occasion. I love it when they live in the constant flow of my life.

Often this flow is blocked by fear, unbelief, false condemnation and a sense of uselessness. Even though I put my life within them, they feel I couldn't use them to convey that life to others. They listen to the deceiver who says they don't have the necessary qualifications or resources. All the time my life wants to burst free from within them.

You see, my child, when I come to live in someone I don't want to be a prisoner locked up in darkness. I want to break free, to pour out of them as rivers of living water; not a trickle, but rivers.

I love changing lives with my life. It doesn't matter how depraved, hurt or broken a life has been, I am able to heal and deliver. I love to rescue those who have reached the gutters of life. I love to see the transformation that new birth brings to the desperate. I love to see the humble seeking for more of my life. I love to see those who are rich in the eyes of this world recognise their spiritual poverty. My child, I love to give my abundant life!

133

The Garden

———— o ————

The garden was obviously neglected; weeds abounded. The land looked useless, totally unproductive. A certain man looked with interest at this piece of land every time he passed. He saw in his imagination not a wasteland of weeds, but glorious fertile soil bringing birth to a great harvest of crops.

One day the owner stood on the piece of land as the man passed by. 'What a wonderful piece of land,' said the man.

The owner looked at him with satisfaction. 'Then this land is now yours,' he replied.

'Mine?' exclaimed the man.

'Yes,' said the owner. 'I'm giving it to you. Everybody else who has passed has seen only weeds and has complained about this land being neglected. But you have a vision of what you can make of this land; so I am happy to entrust it to you. I know you will pull out the weeds and make it abundantly fruitful.'

134

Praise Me

—— o ——

L isten to this. I don't like the narrow confines that many believe are my limitations. The way I lead is narrow so that you escape the corruption of the world. **But that narrow way is full of life.** I delight in everything good and wholesome. Those who walk close to me along that way walk in the fullness of my life.

Because you know me and have received that life, praise springs up from your heart. The life within you bursts forth with praise and adoration. You can't keep quiet, can you? You even praise me in difficult situations.

Don't feel you have to be so polite and restrained in praising me. If you have a praising, joyful, dancing heart, then be free to express what is in you. Don't worry about what others think. Remember liberty is the work of my Spirit!

Some people fill their lives with petty restrictions and lead others into legalistic bondage. They want me to free others when I am longing to break the bondage in their own lives.

135

Don't Limit Me

———— o ————

I hate it when people try to make me religious. They restrict me within their ecclesiastical systems and tell me that I have to work within the confines of their services. Usually I am only allowed one hour. And then precious few really expect me to do anything! If anyone was to receive fullness of life in the middle of the service he would be dismissed as an emotional freak.

But I see the hearts of those who worship me, even in such situations. **I love them all and I listen to their hearts.** So if one cries to me in repentance, I respond immediately. If one cries out in desperation, I am there to comfort. If I see genuine faith, I am ready to answer.

But I am expected to attend so many boring services. You should hear some of the sermons I have to listen to! If I believed what was said I would cease to exist as the God that I am. But I persevere and don't give up. **I give full measure to all who put their trust in me.**

However, you must know that I am angry with leaders who know of my life but don't enable my people to receive it. Some even prevent and hinder them from receiving. They are accountable to me for their actions.

Every congregation of my people should be abounding with my life, overflowing with love for one another – a company of true joy. Instead I continually see compromise. Even in some churches where the truth is proclaimed, it is not allowed to be expressed. Doesn't it annoy you that people prefer mediocrity, lifelessness and formalism to the fullness of my life? Doesn't it sadden you, my child? What are such people afraid of?

I don't want you to judge others. Take my life to them. Don't be deterred if they shut their religious doors in your face. I know what that feels like myself. I have many of them slammed in my face daily.

136

True Worship

—— o ——

I always go where I am wanted. I always work, even within the limitations put on me by men. How frustrating it is to have so much life, yet be unable to share it with multitudes who are ignorant of what I offer them. I work within ecclesiastical systems despite their problems and restrictions. I work outside these institutions also. Wherever my people gather in my name I am there in their midst. And I rejoice in all who welcome me.

I hate it when my children are jealous of one another, or imagine they are the only ones I know and bless. I hate it when they speak against one another. I don't speak against those who are bound by religious traditionalism or write them off. I love them and want to liberate them by revealing the truth. **I want them to have the fullness of my life.**

Worship must be in spirit and truth. It is not a sweet presentation of music, but the expression of love in the hearts of my people that gives me such pleasure. I want to influence every area of their lives, their minds and decisions, their homes and relationships. I want to be involved in their use of time and money, their work and recreation. I want them to enjoy life to the full, like I do! I want them to enjoy life with me because I am with them. My child, I love life!

137

True Prayer

———— o ————

My dear child, my heart reaches out to you every day. This is why I want you to spend time with me daily. I love it when we can talk together, especially when you open your heart to me. You don't always do that, do you? Sometimes you say the things you think you ought to say, the things you imagine I want to hear. But you don't say what you really mean, what is in your heart. You think I wouldn't approve if you did.

Now listen, I much prefer you to speak the truth from your heart. Tell me how it really is with you. I don't mind. You see, I know already. **I know what is in your heart;** so what point is there in trying to conceal it from me? That seems futile. And it doesn't please me to listen to a whole lot of false pleasantries. That may sound like prayer to you, but it doesn't to me!

Sometimes I hear you praying with others and it sounds as if you are speaking more to them than to me. You are so concerned about whether they approve your prayer that you forget who you are talking to. Many times your heart has been bursting with a real prayer, but you have held back and remained silent in case the others didn't approve. What a pity!

How I love it when people stop performing and become really honest with one another as well as with me. I wish there were more prayer meetings like that. Sometimes hardly an honest word is spoken in the whole meeting. People spar with one another; they fence, even in prayer. They correct each other's doctrine and criticise each other. How can I answer prayer like that? What am I to answer?

I know how critical and judgmental Christians can be; I am on the receiving end enough to know that! So I understand your reasons for wanting to remain silent. I don't want the critics running my church. I want those who are open to be led by my Spirit and to encourage you, and others like you, to walk boldly and confidently in my Spirit.

138

Humble and Confident

———— o ————

There have been times when I wanted to speak through you but you haven't dared to speak in case others disapproved. You have been afraid of being wrong or mishearing what I've said. I don't punish you on such occasions; but I am sad because I really want you to trust the Holy Spirit to speak through you. It doesn't matter whether others approve. Better to please me than men.

I know you are put off by those who are always speaking out and making contributions, especially those who seem to pray those beautiful, eloquent prayers. Well, I want you to know that the simple prayer of your heart is as beautiful to me as any other prayer.

I love the humble approach. Mind you, I don't want grovelling. I like you to come humbly but confidently. I am your Father. No Father wants a snivelling, grovelling child.

I appreciate that my children have many styles of praying. I don't mind that because I like variety. Some are very brash in their approach. It surprises people that I quite like that. Often there is real faith behind such prayer and **I always honour faith.** Such people receive very positive answers.

I like my children to be bold and confident, even though they are to be humble and gracious. If that brashness oversteps the mark and becomes pride then I have to take measures to humble that child. But whether the style is loud or quiet, what matters is that the prayer comes from the heart.

There is nothing false or superficial about me. Jesus hated hypocrisy and expressed my loathing of it. But I love honesty. I am glad, therefore, when my children are honest.

139

Full of Joy

—— o ——

My dear child, I want to tell you how much I rejoice in you. It grieves me that so many of my children do not really believe I enjoy them. They are constantly distracted by their inadequacies. They imagine I look at them with a frown instead of a smile.

Think of the joy a father and mother have when their child is born. **What great joy I had when you were born again!** I caused all heaven to rejoice. Heaven could only rejoice in you because I rejoiced.

I want my joy to be in you and your joy to be full. Many of your inhibitions have gone, haven't they? I love to break through all that stuff. It's great when you want to skip and dance and rejoice with me. This is my joy in you. Don't you realise that I was already rejoicing before it even occurred to you?

Joy is not an emotional response to situations. I am not an emotion; I am Spirit. **Joy is a fruit of my Spirit in your life.** I don't want to see that joy suffocated by problems and cares that concern you.

I never take my joy away from you. It is always within you and can always be expressed in your life.

140

My Surprises

———— o ————

I don't take delight in everything you do. At times you rightly expect to be disciplined. But on other occasions I surprise you. Instead of punishing you, I give to you and cause you to rejoice. You have thought, 'Why should that happen? What have I done to deserve this?' Nothing, my child. I like surprising you. I only reprimand you when necessary. I achieve much better results when I bless you; you are motivated to obey me when I encourage you. Not many people would like me if I was only interested in correcting them. Those who think I am never satisfied have a very false view of me. I am very different from that, as you well know!

People are filled with joy when they meet with me, when they are born again, filled with my Spirit, healed or when they receive an important answer to prayer. On such occasions they are so thankful. This is why I love to do these things in their lives. I love to see their joy and receive their thanks.

141

Rejoice Always

——— o ———

I know what you are wondering. If I am the God who desires such joy in my children, why do they experience so many things that are a denial of my joy?

When my Son came and lived among you, his joy raised him above others. But his life was not easy. He was constantly rejected and mistreated, ridiculed and persecuted. But he never lost his joy.

I understand the difficulties in your life. I know the tensions, problems, opposition and the ridicule you face because you believe in me. Didn't I say that in the world you would have trouble?

You have begun to discover that **if you praise and rejoice in me in the midst of the difficulties, my power is released in the situation**. Things may not change immediately but your perspective certainly changes, and you begin to realise that I am much bigger than the problem. Then you know I am able to meet the need.

My child, giving thanks in all circumstances is a real act of faith. I love to see my people walking by faith and trusting me.

You have come through many difficulties, moments of darkness and despair. You have been afraid and overcome by a sense of failure. You have felt judged and criticised.

Do you remember what I said to you in such times? 'Rejoice!' Sometimes you've argued with me, haven't you? 'I don't feel like rejoicing. I can't rejoice. It would be unreal if I did.' I tell you to rejoice always! And my Spirit will encourage you to do so.

Rejoice in my generosity. Rejoice in me, my child. I rejoice in you – and in giving to you. Why not rejoice in receiving from me?

142

I Am Holy

———— o ————

My dear child, I am holy. I sense your reaction immediately. I know how afraid you have been of my holiness. Yet I am holy by nature. My love is holy. My grace, mercy, righteousness, truth and faithfulness are all expressions of my holiness. You are afraid only because you don't understand the true nature of my holiness.

I know you are longing to be in heaven with me. You will be able to enjoy me without all the temptations and problems caused by the world, the flesh and the devil. Did you know heaven is the place of my holiness? Those who surround my throne acknowledge me as holy. There is no sin, fear, shame, guilt, sickness or pain. All the host of heaven rejoices and praises me. They have a wonderful time because they can enjoy my holiness unhindered.

You see, holiness is great! It brings tremendous happiness into the lives of my children. Unholiness mars their real enjoyment of me.

Are you beginning to get the idea? Holiness is not something to dread but to long for, just as you long for heaven. In fact these two things are one and the same. **If you long for heaven you long for holiness, and if you long for holiness you long for heaven.**

I am leading you towards the fulfilment of my promises. I will raise you at the last day and you will reign with me in glory. This is why I want you to be holy as I am holy. This is not merely a pleasant wish; it is essential. Only the holy can inhabit heaven. Without holiness no one will see me.

143

Heaven is Yours

—— o ——

Your fears originate because you think of yourself as unholy and you are afraid of judgment. Many passages in the Bible indicate that men suffer terrible affliction when I judge them in my holiness. Yes, it is true – there are harsh judgments awaiting the unholy.

If you belonged to the world and not to me, you would have every justification to be afraid of confronting me in my holiness. But as it is, there is no need to fear. I want to reveal myself to you in my holiness. This will not be a devastating experience for you, but a wonderful one. If you belonged to the kingdom of darkness you would need to shy away from holiness. You would not want the light of my truth to shine into the inner recesses of your being.

But I have saved you from the dominion of darkness and have already made you a child of my Kingdom. This Kingdom is within you. Do you hear what I am saying, child? **You already have the gift of heaven.** It is birthed within you.

As I work in you by the power of my Spirit, so I am causing the holy life of heaven to be expressed more fully in you. I myself, in my holiness, am being lived out in your life.

When my holiness comes up against the unholy, fleshly desires, you experience conflict. You make the mistake of thinking those desires disqualify you from my holiness. They don't. If they did, every one of my children would be disqualified from heaven. So I want to put that fear in the dustbin where it belongs.

144

You Are Holy

—— o ——

Remember what I have done for you in my holiness.
Jesus gave his holy life to cleanse you from all your
unholiness. I have put my Spirit within you; he is holy.
**You have the Holy One living within you, child. You are
made holy in my sight. You are sanctified. I have
cleansed you of your unholiness.**

I call you my dear child because you are dear to me. But
I could also call you my holy child – a saint. Isn't that
extraordinary? You are a saint. That means you are one
who is sanctified, called by me and set apart for my
purposes.

When you were born again I gave you the gift of
eternal life because I wanted you for myself. **To be holy is
to be set apart for me.** Obviously, if you are set apart for
me, you are also set apart from sin and the devil's
dominion, from fear and injustice. You are set apart *from*
all that is evil and set apart *for* all that is good. Isn't that
wonderful?

Why be afraid of my holiness when it means that you
are saved and set apart for all that is good? Isn't the devil
a liar? He wants you to imagine you still belong to him,
instead of me. Those who belong to me inherit my holy
life and will reign with me here in heaven. I am looking
forward to having you here with me.

Listen, dear one, I didn't set you apart only to lose you somewhere along the way. I will certainly bring you to the fulfilment of what I have planned for you. That's encouraging, isn't it?

145

A Holy Life

———— o ————

I know your heart. There is that element of striving within you. You think you will only arrive in heaven if you do everything right. Well, it doesn't work like that. You will be in heaven because I have already done the right things for you. You can rejoice in that.

Don't misunderstand me. I am not suggesting that it doesn't matter what you do now. **Because you are holy I want you to live a holy life.**

Oh, there we go again. Fear! This fear is very deeply ingrained in you, isn't it? Every time I tell you that I expect holiness in your life you get very fearful. Let me ask you a question. Who lived the holy life, I mean a perfect holy life? That's right – Jesus. Was he miserable? No! The anointing of joy upon him raised him above his companions. Was he fearful, depressing or legalistic? Did he restrict people so much that they avoided his presence? No! Only the traditionalists wanted to avoid him because they were content with a formal kind of religion. Those who recognised their need were attracted by his holiness.

Now I am going to say something that will surprise you. I am going to work out my holiness in you so that you are really attractive as a person. As with Jesus, some religious ones are going to feel very awkward about your holiness; it will be a challenge to them.

I am going to make you more and more like Jesus, changing you from one degree of his glory to another. You are going to become more loving, joyful, faithful, peaceful, patient, kind, generous and gentle! You will be full of faith and able to exercise his power and authority in greater measure.

This is not a bad idea, is it? Why be fearful of such things? Don't you want to be like that? You think it's impossible? Well, just remember who is speaking to you! Nothing is impossible for me. I am able to work this out in you because I am who I am! Good news?

146

Co-operate With Me

———— o ————

Now, my dear child, as with so many things I do in your life, I do require your co-operation if you are going to live in holiness. I have given you a holy nature, but you have to let that life be worked out through your daily experience. Don't try to be holy by your own efforts. You cannot put on a performance of holiness for the benefit of others. No, **allow my holy life to shine through you.** Out of your innermost being rivers of living water will flow, the rivers of my holiness in you. Isn't that wonderful?

I love to see the fruit of my Spirit growing in you. I rejoice to see the gifts of my Spirit being used by you. All these activities of my Spirit are aspects of my holiness. The fruit is holy; the gifts are holy. And both are working in you! So there is more of my holiness shining through your life than perhaps you realise!

147

Resist the Liar

———— o ————

I know what concerns you – it's the unholy parts, isn't it? You think that a few unholy thoughts disqualify you from enjoying my holiness. My Spirit in you is much bigger, more impressive and powerful than a few puny thoughts!

It is time you were aware of the enemy's tactics. You see, because I have given you a holy life, there is nothing he can do to take that holiness away from you. He can't steal your new birth or your eternal inheritance. So he tries to prevent you from enjoying your life with me. He attempts to deceive you into thinking that you are not really accepted and couldn't possibly be holy.

He does this by planting unholy thoughts in your mind and encouraging fleshly attitudes. I've watched him do it. You have fallen for his tactics again and again, haven't you? Instead of resisting the enemy, you have thought yourself a terrible failure. Then he accuses you in an attempt to make you feel condemned. He suggests you are not holy. How could you be holy with such thoughts and attitudes?

Unfortunately, my child, you have agreed with him sometimes. But now you understand the source of these thoughts, you can stand against them. You don't have to put up with any of his lying tactics.

Oh, I know what you are thinking. It's not just the thoughts, but the desires that concern you. I know, I know; but the thoughts give birth to the desires. This is why the enemy feeds these thoughts to you again and again. When the thoughts become desire, you lose your resolve to stand against them. Then you are more likely to yield to temptation. Along comes the enemy again with his condemning thoughts: 'See how unholy you are. Look what you have done. A true child of God, sanctified and called to be a saint, wouldn't do anything like that.' Don't believe his lies.

Listen, my dear child. I have saints all over the world. I have millions of children, and they all sin. They all fail me and do unholy things. They are all aware of the same kind of conflicts that rage within you. I don't allow this to disqualify them from the inheritance I have chosen to give them. I have to teach each one of them personally not to believe the lying deceptions of the evil one, but to believe the revelation of my truth.

If anyone knows who is holy, it is me! So don't argue with me any more. **If I say you are holy, you are holy!** Because you are holy, you are called to be holy. If you believe you are unholy, you will certainly do unholy things. But if you believe you are holy because of all I have done for you, then you will live the Jesus life, won't you? Not perfectly. You have not yet reached the stage of perfection. There is a long, long way to go before you are at that stage!

148

You Have Made Progress

——— o ———

Let us consider this together for a moment. You are more loving than you used to be, aren't you? Before you were born again and part of my Kingdom, you didn't love in the way you do now. I wonder where that love came from!

You are certainly happier now than when you walked in this world's ways, even though sometimes you are disappointed with yourself when you fail me. You are more peaceful. You lose that peace when you worry, but it is restored when you trust me. **You have made progress, child.**

And lots of your prayers have been answered, haven't they? You see, there goes the enemy again. He points out all the ones that apparently haven't been answered. Remember those that have. You have faith and trust in my word now, don't you? This is more progress!

Consider your relationships. I know you still find these hard at times. Some people are really difficult to love, aren't they? But you are not as judgmental as you used to be, neither are you so critical. Some people you love now, you could not have loved before. That is progress.

All this is progress in the sanctifying work of my Spirit. These things have not happened by your own effort. They are my work in you. Aren't you encouraged, child?

149

Be Holy

——— o ———

Now, my child, I have something serious to say to you. Encouraging you to be holy is the most important thing I am doing in your life. So I do want you to turn away from those sins. You know the ones I mean. They are a constant contradiction to the life of Jesus in you, aren't they? You don't have to give in to such temptations, you know. Sometimes you feel the pressure will only be relieved if you indulge yourself.

The trouble is, if you indulge yourself once, you want to indulge yourself again and again. Then you get caught in a trap. That sin becomes part of you, and you lose the desire to be set free from it. So I have to speak a strong word to you to bring you to your senses. In my holy love, I discipline all my children for their good.

I am very tolerant. I wait until you realise you need to be set free from this pattern of behaviour and the attitudes which displease me.

You see, when you lose your appetite for sin, you really want to be set free from it. Then I can act. I have had a lot of experience in dealing with children like you. I deal with you at very close quarters because I live *in* you. I know you so well, child. I know how you think and react. **I don't live in you as a divine spy, but to enable you to enjoy my life.**

150

I Came

——— o ———

My dear child, I am a holy God. But in my Son I was not afraid to come among the unholy to touch their lives with my holiness. You see, I make the unholy clean, but the unholy can never tarnish me.

Jesus was not afraid that he would be corrupted or yield to temptation. He was tempted in every way that you are, and yet he never sinned. He could share every experience, except sin. He mixed with the prostitutes, outcasts and sinners, touching the corrupt with his holy love and power.

You see, in love he came as a servant and washed the disciples' feet. He didn't come with a blast of trumpets and with great acclamation that the King of heaven was now walking on earth. **He came and lived the life my children had to live, expressing holiness in the midst of a corrupt and perverse world.**

He gathered around him disciples who knew the same kind of dilemmas and conflicts that you experience. He had to be very patient with them while he trained and taught them, just as I have to be patient with you.

Some people think that he cannot really have enjoyed his humanity, but he loved it. Even though there was rejection, persecution, and people often met him with unbelief and ridicule, nevertheless, he really enjoyed being human. He had to leave his divine glory so that he could become life-size.

He didn't enjoy the process of crucifixion, but went joyfully to the cross because he knew what the outcome of his sacrifice would be. He reached out to people when they needed healing and help. He taught them from my heart. He enjoyed it. It was hard work, mind you. He got tired, just like everybody else; and sometimes the lack of faith in his disciples was very frustrating. But he fulfilled his task; and so I am able to welcome you into my Kingdom.

151

The Devil Defeated

——— o ———

I demonstrated how holiness can be lived out in a human being. That was fun. The devil thought he would catch Jesus out at some point. He tried hard enough in the wilderness! He thought he had what he wanted when he saw him hanging on the cross. I can hear his shriek of anguish when he suddenly realised he was defeated! All his demonic powers were overcome because **Jesus offered me a perfect sacrifice, uncontaminated by any evil.**

I even enjoyed sending Jesus to Hades to preach to the departed. It was good to take my holiness there. They needed it. These are things that many of my children never even stop to ponder.

152

Go in My Holiness

———— o ————

Now, my child, just as I came among men in my holiness, so I am sending you among them in your holiness. I don't want you to tuck yourself away in some kind of spiritual prison. I want to see my children where the action is! **Purity is best demonstrated by generosity,** by giving freely what you have received freely. I want you to radiate my holy joy where it matters.

Don't be afraid of what the religious ones say. They opposed me and they will oppose you. Go where there is need, where people want help and are longing to be set free. Take my holiness into the gutters and ghettos. Take my love where people have lost hope and don't know which way to turn.

I draw you close to me to encourage and strengthen you. I want you to know tender moments when I express my affection for you. Then you will be aware of my love and faithfulness, no matter where I lead you.

Many think of holiness only in terms of behaviour patterns. They look at others through their spiritual magnifying glasses to see whether everything is morally correct. I wish they would turn their magnifying glasses on their own hearts!

Holiness includes righteousness but is much greater than moral behaviour. **It includes obedience to my word, going in my name to those who need me.** I bless those who reach out to others with my love. I encourage them and provide abundantly for them.

153

My Holy Judgment

——— o ———

My dear child, I am no longer among you as a human; now I reign in glory. The whole host of heaven proclaims my holiness. You often feel unworthy to come before my throne because you regard it not only as the seat of my majesty, but also of judgment. But the blood of my Son has cleansed you of your unworthiness. Now you can worship me because you are truly accepted.

I will judge nations in my holiness. Those who continue in rebellion and unrighteousness can expect to reap the reward they deserve. In my holiness I cannot condone sin. I cannot treat rebellion lightly. It is not my desire to condemn anyone. Two things will happen when people come before my judgment seat and are confronted by my holiness. My children will rejoice, for this will be the fulfilment of their longing to know me as I really am. Their hope to be transformed into my likeness will be realised when they see Jesus face to face.

Judgment will be fearful for those who have rejected holiness. My anger and punishment will be on those who fight against the truth and walk in their own ways with stubborn hearts. **If people don't desire holiness on earth, they don't belong in heaven.** They would only be out of place.

I long, therefore, to see stubborn hearts and minds changed by the power of my Spirit. My kindness and mercy is meant to lead to repentance. I never stop speaking words of faith where there is unbelief. I want my people to hear, to turn to me in repentance and receive the life I offer them.

How many really want holiness? How many want to please me? I wish there were more, don't you?

You don't need to live with a fearful sense of judgment hanging over you. You have passed from death to life. You are my child, my holy child, a child of my Kingdom, in whom I delight.

154

Holiness is Wholeness

———— o ————

My dear child, **holiness is wholeness**. This means I want you to be healthy in every way – spirit, soul and body. I want my holy life to touch every part of you.

My Holy Spirit has lived in you ever since you were born again. I want your mind to be consecrated to me and set upon things that are wholesome, for you to be free from negative thinking. I want you to enjoy my holiness, to feel my love for you instead of being bound by fear and feelings of unworthiness. I want your will to be submitted to my will. I want you to be careful how you use your body because it is a temple of my Holy Spirit, a sanctuary of my holy presence.

I want your body to enjoy me. I want your soul to enjoy love. **My holy love will bring you real joy, happiness and fulfilment.** But if you step outside my boundaries, this will bring tension, confusion and fear.

I am always with you and I will never allow you to be tempted beyond that which you are able to endure. You are always able to say 'No', my child. Being tempted gives you an opportunity for victory. Temptation strengthens you when you resist it.

If there are some occasions when you fail and yield to temptation, don't be too discouraged. All my children fail at times. When you yield to temptation, I don't throw you out of my Kingdom. I wait for you to turn back to me in repentance. Then I cleanse and restore you.

155

I Always Do What Is Right

———— o ————

Think of my righteousness as being the very best for you. Sometimes my children think they know better than me, and opt for the joy of the moment instead of obedience to my word. They enjoy themselves for a while, but afterwards realise I knew what was best.

I am very patient while this process is taking place. I have to be, because sometimes it takes my children a long time to work through all the things they want to do before they are prepared to do what I want.

I always judge with righteousness. I don't assess things, weighing up one thing against another to see which is the lesser of two evils. I always see to the heart of the matter. I don't simply judge the outward action but the motive and intention that lies behind it.

Because I am righteous, I have always done what is right in your life. I have never done anything unrighteous to you. The enemy has attacked you, and others have dealt with you unrighteously at times. This wasn't my work, so don't blame me! I put things right and restore you.

156

True Righteousness

——— o ———

Many make up their own rules and regulations. This is a form of self-righteousness. They disobey my specific orders, but require obedience to their traditions. In the name of righteousness, some put people under false restrictions which I haven't placed upon them. They imagine that what *they* think is righteous must be righteous in my eyes.

You have had experience of this, haven't you, child? You have listened to respected men, more experienced than you, who have given the impression that my righteousness is harsh, restricting and virtually impossible to accomplish. You now see that some of these ideas are inconsistent with my heart. **I am much more tender, compassionate, loving and gracious than men!** You see, my dear child, I want right heart attitudes as well as right behaviour.

Love righteousness as I do. I love what is right. Love justice, truth and peace and reach out to others and be willing to get your hands dirty in the world's affairs. I want you to reach those who are depraved, unlovely and seemingly unlovable.

This to me is true righteousness; but the self-righteous will not go to such people. I am angry with those who have no care or compassion for the lost, poor, needy or desperate. Some religious people are like that. Some worldly people are the same. Their actions will determine their reward.

I have freed you in many ways. Now I want you to take my truth to others so that they can be liberated. Will you do that for me, child? Will you take my truth where there is deception, deceit, fear, unbelief and unrighteousness? Will you allow me to declare that truth through you so others are set free? Because you are so thankful for what I am doing in your life, you will do this for me, won't you? Thank you, child.

157

Liberty and Licence

———— o ————

My truth sets people free, not only from sin but from legalism. My Son became a curse to deliver people from the curse of the law. Why are people so legalistic? Because they are afraid of freedom. They fear that liberty will lead to licence. Both legalism and licence are sinful in my sight. I desire liberty for my children, the liberty that can only be expressed by living the truth.

To live in true liberty you need to depend on my grace. You have to love me and my ways more than yourself. When people box themselves up in legalistic attitudes they don't need to depend on my grace. They don't have to exercise faith in me.

It is much easier to live in prison, where everything is provided for you, than to live in the world. But I don't want my children living in prison. I have provided the truth to set them free.

Religious people judge those who fall into sexual sin and temptation. They imagine these to be the worst sins in my sight. How little they know and understand my heart.

You only have to examine my word to see how mightily I can use those who once fell into moral sin, but whose hearts belong to me. This does not mean I condone their sin; but I don't condemn them for it. I restore them when they turn back to me. I don't remove my call on their lives.

If I was to dismiss every one of my children for their moments of rashness and failure, who could I use? Men have so often concentrated on the failure and have missed my heart. I will always forgive when my children truly repent and turn from their sin.

My dear child, men won't like it when you speak like this because they don't like it when I speak in such ways. That is why so many rejected Jesus and the things he said. You see, men judge me as well as you. Those with harsh, hard and judgmental hearts try to make me like them. They constantly bring others under judgment and condemnation while I am trying to encourage them. They even imagine they are doing my will. They weary me. I love them but they weary me.

In the parable, the unmerciful servant received forgiveness and love, but then judged his fellow servant. He acted in unrighteousness and was judged by his own actions.

Those who apply judgmental passages of scripture to others always seem to excuse themselves. Did Jesus want to come in righteous indignation into the temple with a whip? How many times had he already been into the temple with words of compassion, forgiveness, life and truth? How many times did he bring healing and deliverance? His righteous act of judgment was a last resort.

The self-righteous ones, the traditionalists and re-ligious legalists take no account of my heart. They think outward conformity satisfies me. I long for people to know more of my heart. I want to fill their hearts with my merciful forgiveness, my tender compassion and my gracious love. **Don't judge others, child – love them.**

158

Lord of Glory

——— o ———

My dear child, I am the Lord of glory. I alone am worthy of honour and praise. I am bathed in inexpressible light, a radiance beyond anything you could envisage.

Jesus emptied himself of the glory that was his in heaven. He had to reveal my glory in what he said, and he did this so that you could comprehend it. He didn't come to glorify himself but to honour me through his obedience. He walked in holiness and righteousness, justice and truth.

He didn't seek his own self-esteem. He drew men to me and to my Kingdom. **Jesus was the human expression of my glory.** He deserves all the praise and honour you can give him. He is the Lamb in the midst of my throne, reigning in majesty and glory. Draw near to me; come before my throne with a sincere heart and in full assurance of faith. This is where you belong – in my glory.

159

My Glory in You

———— o ————

I want your words and works to glorify me, child. You
don't radiate my glory in the full way Jesus did, and I
don't expect that. But through my Spirit working in you I
am transforming you into my likeness from one degree of
glory to another.

It is true, my child, that ever-increasing glory is being
reflected in your life. This happens in a number of
different ways. My presence within you radiates through
your face, your body, your life-style. You reveal my glory
in a dark and sinful world.

I want you to know that the cloud of my glory over-
shadows you. You never need to live under a cloud of
oppression or darkness when you can live under the
cloud of my glory. Wherever you go, that cloud goes
with you. My divine glory is your inheritance.

You can do glorious things at any time and in any
place, even when you feel you have nothing to give. The
words you speak with boldness and confidence as revelation from my heart bring me glory. When you step
out in faith, trusting my word, you bring me glory. When
you confront sinners with their need to repent, reaching
out to the lost with my love, you bring me glory. When
you obey the leading of my Spirit and do what I ask, you
give me glory. There are already many ways in which I

am glorified through you, although there is always room for improvement.

You would like an experience of my glory, wouldn't you, child? Do you expect to see a cloud of glory, or to be enveloped in some kind of mystical experience? Such things happen, but **my glory is reflected in the way you reveal Jesus to others.**

In this way, you *add* to my glory. And that is even more important than receiving a revelation of my glory. Don't you think it is a great privilege, child, to be able to add to my glory every day? I think that's wonderful. This is why I have called and chosen you.

You will add to my glory in the future and in heaven. You will stand among the redeemed and proclaim my glory, honour and praise, I shall hear your voice and be pleased. You will experience my glory eternally!

160

The Reward Outweighs the Cost

———— o ————

I want you to live in the hope of glory. No matter what you experience now, glory awaits you. Jesus will come again as the Lord of glory. Beyond this life you will come into the full radiance of my glory that at present you only know partially. When you see me face to face, you will be transformed into my likeness. This will be the completion of what I have planned and my glory will be reflected perfectly in you.

I promise that you will share in my glory, provided you share in the sufferings of Jesus while you are on earth. **The cost of following me is nothing compared to the glory that is to be revealed in you.** I will give glory, honour and peace to those who obey me. The reward far outweighs the cost, child.

There are always those who seek glory without cost. They want reward but are not prepared for obedience. Every man will be rewarded for what he has done.

My deepest sorrow about sin is that it deprives people of the glory I desire for them. All have sinned and fallen short of this glory. I grieve over those who are deceived because they follow false gods and miss the glory that could be theirs if they put their faith in Jesus. But I rejoice in all who receive salvation from me. You are a child of my glory. I see you already seated in heavenly places in Jesus.

I was also glad in your death and the rich welcome I gave you into my eternal Kingdom. It may surprise you to hear me say this. You see, my child, in my eyes this has already happened. I know it lies in the future as far as you are concerned, but I can see the end from the beginning. And I know you will enjoy me eternally as much as I enjoy you.

161

Child of Glory

—— o ——

My dear child, your destiny is assured. I see you already reflecting my glory in the way I have planned. I see my purpose fulfilled, even while it is being worked out. I see you walking in my ways, resisting temptation. I see you affirming your faith in me and reaching out to others, seeking first my Kingdom and my righteousness. I see the rich reward that awaits you and I rejoice.

I regard you as a child of glory, not as a child of the earth. You are now working for things that last, not the things that will pass away.

Don't see yourself as purely human, but in terms of the destiny that awaits you. It is worth working for my Kingdom and putting me first, isn't it, beloved child?

162

You Glorify Me

———— o ————

I am thankful you don't mind paying the cost of being faithful. Listen carefully to me, child. Does it surprise you to know that I, your Lord and God, am thankful to you? You have always been the one to give me thanks. There have been few occasions when you have allowed me to thank you.

You glorify me by the way my love pours out of you to others, by the time you give to them, the affection you share with them and your concern in praying for them. I am glorified because you have wanted to be more effective in loving and ministering to others. You have glorified me with your praises.

I love to see you rejoicing in me, glad that you are alive in Jesus. I love to see your heart skipping and dancing – and your body, too!

You glorify me in the way you resist temptation, when you refuse the offers of the world, the flesh and the devil. I rejoice when you deny yourself, take up your cross and follow me. **Every act of self-denial in your life has added to my glory,** when you have obeyed me out of love. It is better to obey grudgingly than not at all; but you only add to my glory when you obey out of love.

My child, I know the sacrifices you have made, the cost you have faced. I know also the longing in your heart.

You love me so much, you long for more of me. Listen child, you add to my glory even by your longing. I will reward you.

163

Cycles of Growth

———— o ————

You have often condemned yourself for not living constantly in the full flow of revelation from me. I have watched you agonise over this. I have tried to comfort you but you have found it difficult to receive my words of truth.

Once you have tasted the best, nothing less is good enough, is it? But I give you this promise, child. You will know other times like this. Throughout your life there will be periods of exceptional blessing. Don't be disappointed that you are unable to live on the mountain top all the time.

My dear child, do you find this difficult to receive? You do realise that I use you at all times, not only when you experience exceptional blessing. The other times encourage you to seek me and to pray for revival. You would like to live in heaven on earth, wouldn't you?

Let me remind you what Jesus said. Every fruitful branch is pruned to make it more fruitful still. You have these glorious periods of fruitfulness, followed by times of pruning when I deal with selfish things such as pride, wrong motivation and disobedience. Then follow periods of growth, which lead to seasons of further fruitfulness and blessing. This is a continuous cycle.

The fact that I take you through seasons of pruning is evidence that I love you and that you are already fruitful. Yet I have heard your complaints at such times: 'Oh Lord, I am not as fruitful as I was'. Of course you are not, dear foolish child. How can you be so fruitful during the pruning season?

You have to bow to my wisdom, don't you? Remember, Jesus accomplished a great deal in three years. **Allow me to deal with you in the way I know best, and more of my glory will shine through your life; you will be more fruitful than in the past.** I have prepared good works for you to walk in.

164

My Glory in Jesus

—— o ——

My Spirit lived in Jesus and took him through all the stages of his manhood, through the times when he grew in wisdom and through the years of his ministry. He preached about my Kingdom, reached out to heal the sick and delivered those bound by evil spirits. He spoke my word, gave my promises and declared my truth.

My Spirit led him through times of rejection, false accusation and mockery, through every temptation, peril and danger. My Spirit led him through the agony in the Garden of Gethsemane, through the pain of crucifixion. There he yielded his Spirit to me and was victorious over all the principalities and powers of darkness.

I remember the morning I raised Jesus. I had seen the despair in the hearts of those who had followed him. Few of them retained their hope. I saw the darkness that had covered the world but I knew what I would do.

I remember the moment the stone was rolled away. Joy filled my heart as life flowed into the corpse that was my Son. I saw him lay aside the grave clothes, folding them neatly. He walked out into the garden. I saw the unbelief turn to joy in the hearts of my disciples when he appeared to them. I remember the day I raised my Son.

When Jesus returned to the glory of heaven, we sent the Holy Spirit upon all who believed in him. Jesus brings me glory by taking what is mine and declaring it to you. My child, the Spirit of Jesus is within you. This is the victorious, triumphant Spirit who lived in him and saw him through all those experiences.

That same Spirit who lives in you, will lead you victoriously through all the experiences of your life, through all opposition, rejection and pain. My Spirit will take you through death itself into the glory of resurrection. You shall have a new risen body in which to reveal my glory for all eternity.

Jesus has gone before you to prepare a place for you. You will reign with me in my everlasting Kingdom. How I rejoice in this! I am longing for you to come and take your appointed place. I am glad you have my Spirit to lead you in triumph. When Jesus appears, you will receive the crown of glory that will never fade.

Appendix of Bible References

1. I HAVE PERSONALITY
Gen 1:3; Ps 29:3–9; Ps 33:6–9; Jer 23:29; Isa 44:24; Jn 1:1–4,14; 8:30

2. IN MY IMAGE
Deut 32:6b; Gen 1:26–27

3. NO ACCIDENT
Matt 22:36–40; Ps 138:8; Rom 8:28

4. CREATED IN LOVE
Rom 8:15; Eph 1:4; Ps 139:13; Ps 33:13–14; Ps 121:8

5. MY PLAN FOR YOU
Eph 1:4–5,13–14; 2 Cor 3:18; Eph 2:8–9; Titus 3:5

6. MY WAY OF SALVATION
Rev 22:13; Gal 1:3–5; Col 1:13; Acts 4:12

7. I CARE FOR YOU
Jn 1:10–11; Isa 53

8. YOU ARE SAVED
Isa 43:11; 1 Jn 1:9; Eph 1:3

9. LET ME LOVE YOU
Matt 11:29; Eph 2:8; Jer 33:6b; 1 Jn 4:19; Ps 62:1; Isa 30:15

10. THE LOST CHILD

11. I LOVE YOU BECAUSE I LOVE YOU
Jer 31:3; Phil 1:6

12. I LOVE YOU MORE THAN YOU LOVE YOURSELF
1 Jn 3:1; 1 Jn 4:16; Isa 53:5; Isa 49:15

13. DON'T BE AFRAID OF LOVE
Lk 6:19; Heb 12:9–10; Heb 4:13

14. I AM GENTLE WITH YOU
Matt 11:29; Isa 50:5; Lk 22:27; Jn 13:1–17; Ps 46:10

15. I AM YOUR FATHER
Rom 8:14–15; Eph 1:7–8; Ps 130:7

16. YOU MAKE IT DIFFICULT FOR YOURSELF
TO RECEIVE LOVE
Rev 12:10–11; Isa 43:4; Ps 103:10

17. I LOVE THE PERSON YOU REALLY ARE
1 Sam 16:7b; Heb 4:13; Ps 38:9; Rom 5:8; Jn 6:63

18. YOU DON'T NEED TO PRETEND
Eph 4:25

19. YOUR APPEARANCE
1 Sam 16:17b; Jn 7:24; Lk 16:15; Ps 24:3–4; Rom 12:1

20. THE REAL YOU
Ps 45:11; Matt 6:6

21. OUR PRAYER MEETINGS
Phil 4:4–6; Matt 26:41

22. BE OPEN
Ps 62:8; Heb 4:12

23. GIVE AND YOU WILL RECEIVE
Matt 7:2; 2 Cor 9:6

24. NO FEAR IN LOVE
1 Jn 4:18

25. YOU ARE ACCEPTED
2 Cor 6:2; Jn 15:9; Jn 15:13

26. I WATCH OVER YOU
Ps 139:13–16; Rom 11:5

27. PEOPLE
Eph 4:3; Rom 16:1–18; Ps 105:14–15; Matt 6:14

28.   EVERY DETAIL
Lk 12:7; Ps 20:7

29.   I LEAD YOU STEP BY STEP
Phil 2:13

30.   DON'T WORRY ABOUT THE FUTURE
Jer 29:11; Ps 119:105; Matt 6:34; Num 22:28; Jn 16:27

31.   ALL OF ME
Col 2:9–10; Jn 14:15–17; Eph 1:18–19

32.   ALL OF YOU
1 Cor 6:19–20; Rom 12:1–2; 1 Pet 1:18–19; 2 Cor 9:6–11

33.   I AM MERCIFUL
Ps 103:8; Jn 15:2

34.   TRUE LIBERTY
Gal 5:1; Matt 11:29; Lk 6:36; Eph 2:4

35.   WHEN I FORGIVE, I FORGET
Ps 103; Isa 53:5

36.   FORGIVE
Matt 6:12,14–15

37.   THE FIGHT

38.   LOVE IS PATIENT
1 Cor 13:4; 1 Thess 5:14; Eph 4:2

39.   LOVE DOES NOT BOAST
1 Cor 13:4; 1 Cor 1:28–31

40.   LOVE IS KIND
1 Cor 13:5

41.   LOVE COVERS SINS INSTEAD OF EXPOSING THEM
1 Cor 13:5–7; Heb 8:12; Rom 4:7–8

42.   MY SIN RECORD
1 Pet 1:15

43. YOUR SIN RECORD
Isa 1:18

44. LOVE NEVER FAILS
1 Cor 13:7; Ps 13:5; Ps 25:2; 1 Cor 13:12; 1 Cor 15:42–44; Ps 147:11

45. TRUSTING OTHERS
Jn 2:24

46. I HAVE CHOSEN YOU
1 Jn 3:1; Isa 43:1; 2 Cor 5:17; Isa 55:7b; Matt 28:20b

47. I DISCIPLINE IN LOVE
Ps 94:12; Heb 12:10; Matt 6:33; Jn 16:8; 1 Cor 11:32

48. I ENCOURAGE YOUR FAITH
Matt 28:20b; 1 Kings 19:11–13

49. YOU CAN DO WHAT I ASK
Ps 94:9; 2 Kings 18:7a; Phil 4:13; Mk 9:23b, 10:27

50. I NEVER DESPAIR OF YOU
Isa 43:4a

51. MY LOVE MAKES YOU CLEAN
1 Thess 5:23–24; Jn 15:3; James 1:7

52. I ENJOY YOU
SS 2:10; Zeph 3:17

53. ENJOY BEING YOU
Ps 139:7,23–24

54. RECEIVE AND GIVE
Jn 15:5

55. I AM GRACIOUS
Eph 1:3; Matt 7:8

56. CHILD OF MY GRACE
Eph 3:20; 1 Tim 6:17b; Rom 8:32; Ps 37:4

57. I AM GENEROUS
2 Cor 8:7; Lk 6:30,34–35,38

58. THE OLD CAR

59. THE WAY OF LOVE
Phil 2:5; Jn 13:15; Jn 15:10–12; 2 Jn 6; Isa 48:17–18

60. LOVE IN MY NAME
1 Jn 3:16–18; Gal 15:6b

61. A HEART OF LOVE
Gal 2:20; Rom 6:1–14; Eph 2:10; Jn 15:5; Matt 6:10

62. GO IN LOVE
Jn 13:34

63. I GO IN LOVE
Matt 10:1; Lk 14:27–33; Lk 9:2

64. I GO IN YOU
Matt 5:11–12; Isa 42:6–7; Isa 6:8; 1 Cor 12:27–28; Prov 3:6

65. THE RIGHT TIME

66. SPREAD MY LOVE
2 Cor 2:14; Matt 9:36–38

67. MY KINGDOM OF LOVE
Lk 12:32; Lk 17:21; 1 Cor 4:20; 1 Cor 13:1–13; Rom 14:17

68. YOU ARE FILLED WITH MY POWER
Lk 4:38–39; Lk 5:13; Lk 8:27–37,51–56; Jn 2:1–11; Jn 6:5–13;
Matt 8:23–27; Matt 17:24–27; Acts 1:8

69. MY POWER IN LOVE
1 Cor 4:20–21

70. NOT BY MIGHT OR POWER
Gal 5:6; Jn 12:37; Lk 4:4–12

71. I LOVE WORKING MIRACLES
Ps 77:14

72. LET ME CARRY THE BURDEN
Lk 6:19; Matt 12:15; Ps 68:19; 1 Chron 14:10–11a,13–14,16;
1 Chron 15:13

73.   LOVING DIFFICULT PEOPLE
Gal 6:12

74.   BE REALLY FRUITFUL
Jn 15:8

75.   GIVE YOURSELF TIME TO RECEIVE
Prov 4:23; Ps 68:9

76.   I HEAL
Ex 15:26; Matt 12:10; Matt 8:2–3

77.   CAUSES OF SICKNESS
Ps 107:20; Ps 106:13–15,28–29; Jn 14:1; Phil 4:7

78.   I DON'T WANT YOU TO BE SICK
Gal 4:13–14

79.   THE SICK WOMAN

80.   JESUS HEALED
Matt 14:36; Matt 12:15; Isa 53:5

81.   SICKNESS IS DISTRESSING
Prov 4:20–22; Matt 6:10

82.   RECEIVE YOUR HEALING
Matt 19:26; Mk 9:21–24; Matt 6:14–15

83.   I HATE SICKNESS
Isa 57:1–2; 1 Cor 15:55–57

84.   I WAS THERE IN THE NIGHTMARE
Isa 43:2; Matt 27:46; Ps 40:1–3; Prov 12:17–21; Matt 5:43–44;
1 Thess 5:18; 1 Cor 6:7; Ps 43

85.   THE BATTLE BELONGS TO ME
Jer 20:11; Rom 8:37; Isa 54:16–17; 2 Cor 10:5

86.   I AM LIGHT
Jn 8:12; 1 Jn 1:5; Eph 5:8–11; Matt 5:14–16

87.   POWERS OF DARKNESS
Eph 6:12; Jn 8:34; Rom 6:16; Jn 3:19–20

88. I DISPEL THE DARKNESS
2 Cor 11:14–15; Lk 9:42; Col 2:15; Matt 18:18; Isa 35:8–9

89. THE LIGHT OF THE WORLD
1 Jn 4:4; Jn 8:42–44; Col 1:13; Matt 5:16; Isa 41:10

90. LIVE IN FREEDOM
Gal 5:1; Jn 8:36; James 4:7

91. MY SOVEREIGN WILL
Isa 53:8; 1 Jn 5:4

92. THE ENEMY'S TACTICS
2 Cor 2:11; 2 Cor 12:7; Lk 22:31–32; Rom 8:34

93. VICTORY
Lk 9:1–2; Ps 91:11; Jn 12:31; Jn 16:11

94. I AM YOUR SHIELD
Ps 18:2; 1 Pet 5:8; 2 Tim 1:7

95. I HATE DARKNESS
Isa 8:19–20; Nahum 3:4; Eph 5:11–13

96. FIGHT THE GOOD FIGHT
Jn 8:44; 2 Cor 4:4; Jn 16:33; 1 Jn 3:7–8; Ps 44:4–8; Rom 8:37; 1 Jn 5:18–20

97. I AM THE GOD OF JUSTICE
Ps 72:4,12–14

98. IT IS FINISHED
Rom 3:10–12; Rom 6:23; Jn 3:17–18; Jn 19:30

99. MY RIGHTEOUS JUDGMENT
Rom 2:5–8

100. I LOVE EVERYONE
Jer 10:10–12; Isa 45:20–21

101. MY COVENANT PEOPLE
Jn 5:23,39–40; Jn 15:23; Rom 3:20–22; Rom 11:25–32; Matt 24:14

102. THE SON AND I ARE ONE
Jn 10:30; Jn 5:23; Jn 13:20b; Jn 14:6,9; Jn 15:23

103. JUDGING OTHERS
Rom 9:15–16; 1 Sam 16:7; Matt 21:31–32; Jn 8:42–47; Ps 9:4; Jn 8:15; Matt 7:1–2

104. THE FORGIVEN

105. HELL
2 Pet 2:4–10; Rom 6:23; Matt 13:42; Matt 25:30

106. MEN FORM THEIR OWN JUDGMENT
1 Jn 2:16–17; Eph 1:3; Deut 11:26–28; Jn 3:36; Jn 12:47–48; 2 Cor 5:10; Ps 79:6

107. THE NARROW WAY
Lk 11:49–51; Rev 6:9–11; Lk 9:23–26; Matt 7:13–14

108. NOT UNDER WRATH
Eph 2:1–10

109. I AM THE TRUTH
Jn 14:6; 1 Jn 1:5; Jn 1:14; Jn 8:32; Ps 26:2–3

110. THE TRUTH WORKS
1 Cor 2:4–5; Matt 24:35; Lk 8:15; Rom 12:2; Prov 2:1–5; Prov 4:20

111. DON'T JUDGE MY WORD
Jn 6:23; 2 Tim 3:16

112. CLING TO THE TRUTH
Jn 17:17; 1 Thess 5:16–18; Col 3:15; 2 Cor 5:17; Rom 8:1–2; 1 Cor 3:16; Eph 1:6; Rom 8:37–39; Rom 2:11; 2 Pet 1:3; Heb 12:2; Prov 4:20–22

113. THE MAN WITH THE STOOP

114. FEED ON THE TRUTH
Col 3:16

115. THE WALK

116. I AM FAITHFUL
2 Tim 2:13; Matt 24:35; Jer 1:12

117. YOU WANT TO BE FAITHFUL
Jn 14:23 Matt 7:24–27; Ps 18:2,31; 1 Tim 6:17; Ps 103:2–3

118.   DO YOU BELIEVE?
Ps 145:13; Jn 14:13–14; Isa 55:8–9; Lk 11:1–8; Lk 18:1–8; Ps 66:17–20;
Matt 21:22; Ps 37:4

119.   TRUE FAITHFULNESS
Eph 5:17; Mk 11:24; Rom 4:18–21; Lk 8:15; Jn 8:19; Jn 14:7; Jn 17:9–19;
Jn 15:12–13

120.   TRUST ME
James 1:22–25; Phil 1:6; Jude 24

121.   I AM WISDOM
Prov 8:12–31; Isa 11:2; Ps 49:3; James 3:17; Rom 13:14; Matt 5:27–30;
Mk 9:43–47; 2 Cor 10:5; Eph 4:17–24; Heb 4:15

122.   WORDS OF WISDOM
2 Tim 3:16; Jn 6:63,68; Col 3:16; Jn 14:25; James 1:5; James 3:17;
Dan 2:20–23; Prov 12:8; Prov 28:1; Prov 2:6

123.   THIS IS WISDOM
Prov 2:6,9–10; Prov 3:13,17; Isa 32:17; Prov 9:10; Ps 111:10; Prov 28:26;
Prov 11:2; James 3:13; Lk 2:40; Lk 2:52; Ps 119:160

124.   MY AUTHORITY
Col 1:16–17; Job 1:6–12; Job 2:1–6; Ps 47:7–9; Ps 2

125.   MY CRITICS
Rom 2:1–3; Matt 7:21–23; James 4:1

126.   MY AUTHORITY IN JESUS
Mk 1:22; Lk 4:36; Jn 8:28; Jn 5:19

127.   MY AUTHORITY IN YOUR LIFE
Matt 7:21

128.   SUBMIT JOYFULLY
Ps 119:47,56–60; Ps 100:2a; Phil 4:7; 1 Cor 1:5–7; Heb 13:20–21;
Matt 21:21–22

129.   AUTHORITY IN MY CHURCH
Heb 13:17; 1 Tim 3:1–5,9–10

130.   TRUE AUTHORITY IN LEADERS
Jn 12:43; Eph 5:21

131. I GIVE MY LIFE
Ps 27:14; Ps 37:7; Ps 46:10; Matt 20:1–15

132. RECEIVE THE HOLY SPIRIT
Lk 11:9–13; 1 Cor 1:4–7; Jn 7:38–39; Heb 7:25; Rom 8:31–32

133. THE GARDEN

134. PRAISE ME
Jn 10:10b; Gal 3:1–5

135. DON'T LIMIT ME
Heb 4:16; Matt 23:13

136. TRUE WORSHIP
Matt 18:20; Gal 5:13–15; 1 Thess 5:14; Jn 4:23–24

137. TRUE PRAYER
Jn 2:24; Acts 1:24

138. HUMBLE AND CONFIDENT
1 Pet 4:10–11a; Acts 5:29; Lk 18:9–14; Heb 10:19–25; Matt 6:5–8

139. FULL OF JOY
Lk 15:7; Ps 119:111; Ps 19:8; Zeph 3:17

140. MY SURPRISES
Ps 21:6; Ps 126:1–3

141. REJOICE ALWAYS
Heb 1:9; Jn 16:33; James 1:2–4; Acts 16:23–26; 1 Thess 5:16–18;
Phil 4:4–7; Jn 13:3–17

142. I AM HOLY
Isa 6:1–8; Rev 4; Deut 26:15; Jn 6:20; 1 Pet 1:15; Heb 12:14

143. HEAVEN IS YOURS
Jn 3:20–21; Lk 17:21

144. YOU ARE HOLY
Heb 9:14; 1 Cor 6:19; Heb 10:10; 1 Cor 1:2

145. A HOLY LIFE
1 Thess 4:3,7; Heb 1:9; Lk 1:37

146.   CO-OPERATE WITH ME
2 Cor 7:1; Jn 7:38–39; Gal 5:22; 1 Cor 12:1–11

147.   RESIST THE LIAR
2 Cor 2:11; James 4:7; Eph 4:27; James 1:14–15; Deut 14:2; 1 Pet 2:9

148.   YOU HAVE MADE PROGRESS
James 1:18; Jude 24–25

149.   BE HOLY
1 Cor 10:13

150.   I CAME
Jn 1:5; Heb 4:15; Heb 2:18; Matt 18:12–13; Jn 13:1–7; Phil 2:6–11;
Heb 12:2–3

151.   THE DEVIL DEFEATED
Lk 4:1–13; 1 Jn 3:8b; 1 Pet 3:18–22

152.   GO IN MY HOLINESS
Matt 5:14–16

153.   MY HOLY JUDGMENT
Heb 1:3b; Ps 9:7–8; Gal 6:7–8; Jn 3:17–18; Ps 1:5; Jer 2:35; 1 Pet 1:13–16

154.   HOLINESS IS WHOLENESS
Eph 4:17–24; Phil 4:8; 1 Cor 3:16–17; I Cor 10:13; Titus 2:11–12

155.   I ALWAYS DO WHAT IS RIGHT
Heb 12:11; Jn 7:24

156.   TRUE RIGHTEOUSNESS
Phil 3:4–9; Lk 11:46,52; James 2:13b; Isa 61:1–3; Mk 7:5–13; Ps 9:8

157.   LIBERTY AND LICENCE
Gal 3:13–14; Gal 5:1–6; 2 Sam 11:12–25; Ps 51; Rom 14:13;
Matt 18:21–35; Rom 2:3–4; Rom 3:20–22; Rom 14:4

158.   LORD OF GLORY
Ps 24:10; Rev 4:11; Ez 1:26–28; Jn 8:54; Jn 7:18; Heb 10:22

159.   MY GLORY IN YOU
2 Cor 3:18; Ps 34:5; Jn 17:24; Ex 40:34–35; 2 Chron 5:13–14;
2 Chron 7:1–3; 2 Thess 1:11–12; Jn 17:4; Rev 5:13

160.   THE REWARD OUTWEIGHS THE COST
Rom 8:18; 1 Thess 4:16; 1 Pet 4:13–14; Rom 8:17; Matt 16:27; Rom 3:23

161.   CHILD OF GLORY
Phil 3:20; Jn 6:27; 1 Cor 9:25; Matt 6:33

162.   YOU GLORIFY ME
Jn 12:25–27

163.   CYCLES OF GROWTH
Ps 73:25; Jn 15:2; Ps 77:6–13; Eph 2:10

164.   MY GLORY IN JESUS
Mk 14:35–36; Jn 20:6–9; Jn 7:38–39; 1 Cor 15:42–44; Jn 14:2–3;
2 Cor 2:14; James 1:12; 1 Pet 5:4